CONDUCTING CHURCH MEETINGS

POCKET ☒ GUIDE

CONDUCTING CHURCH MEETINGS

JOHN E. BAIRD

ABINGDON PRESS
Nashville

Conducting Church Meetings

Copyright © 1991 by Abingdon Press

All rights reserved.

Second Printing 1992

Library of Congress Cataloging-in-Publication Data

Baird, John E. (John Edward), 1922–
    Pocket guide to conducting church meetings/by John E. Baird.
        p.   cm.
    ISBN 0-687-31682-0 (alk. paper)
    1. Church meetings. 2. Parliamentary practice. I. Title
BV652.15.B35   1991
254'.6—dc20   91-7194

MANUFACTURED IN THE UNITED STATES OF AMERICA

ACKNOWLEDGMENTS

The author wishes to express his gratitude:

To General Henry M. Robert and his heirs who have prepared the successive editions of *Robert's Rules of Order*. This most detailed and complete parliamentary authority has served as the basis for what you read here. Anyone following this book will generally act in harmony with *Robert's Rules*. Page numbers given in this book refer to the *Robert's Rules of Order, 1990 Edition*, published by Scott, Foresman and Company, Glenview, Illinois, and available in most book stores.

To those who have read this manuscript and contributed criticisms and suggestions affecting almost every page. Included are Professor Jack Samosky of California State University, Hayward; Mrs. Alice N. Pohl, Certified Professional Parliamentarian and Accrediting Director of the American Institute of Parliamentarians; Eleanor Baird; and Arthur W. Swarthout. These deserve credit for the virtues of this book. The author alone is responsible for its faults.

To Miss Margaret Painter, teacher and friend, who first introduced the author to parliamentary procedure. The book is dedicated to her.

CONTENTS

CONGRATULATIONS!

CONGRATULATIONS!

They elected you Chair, so most of them must believe you can handle the job. You may not be so certain, particularly as you remember some of the business meetings you have attended. Can anyone possibly know enough parliamentary procedure to keep this group under control? You appreciate the gavel your predecessor handed you. If only you could use it on heads instead of on the lectern!

A visit to your local book store provides you with a copy of *Robert's Rules of Order, 1990 Edition*. Fortunately, you avoided the mistake of buying a cheap reprint of an old edition of Robert's Rules. You bought the 1990 edition, published by Scott, Foresman, with all of its details and helpful explanations, choosing between the hardback and paperback formats. However, you notice it has 657 pages of text, plus introduction and index. Does anyone expect you to learn all that? When can you possibly find time to read all that material, let alone try to master it?

Relax! Think of *Robert's Rules of Order, 1990 Edition* (we'll call it *RONR* from here on) as an encyclopedia. It contains answers to all the parliamentary problems you will ever face, and a lot more. But you would no more set out to read it than you would start to read through the encyclopedia to master all the knowledge in the world, or to read through the dictionary to learn all the possible words in the language. Such details are better left to the specialist. You might feel more comfortable with a professional parliamentarian at your elbow (and we certainly recommend the services of such an expert to any group that can afford one), but a few simple rules will cover 99 percent of the situations you will face. A little basic knowledge, some good common sense, and a proper respect for the ideas and feelings of others will usually see you through.

This book is intended to provide that basic knowledge. I have tried to make it as simple and as readable as possible. Scan it before you try to preside at a meeting. Keep it handy to refresh your memory on basic points. Although simple, it agrees with *RONR* in almost all respects, and you may wish to turn to that authority for further details as various problems arise.

A guidebook can only go so far. You must provide the common sense and the respect for the others in your group. You have been elected to a position of leadership and responsibility, but never forget, it is the meek who are blessed and who inherit the earth (Matt. 5:5).

SOME BASIC PRINCIPLES

No ordinary person could hope to memorize all the rules governing all of the possible situations in a business meeting. In fact, some people will complain that these regulations only add to the confusion. Understand, however, that all of these rules represent nothing more than the application of a few basic principles to meet a great variety of situations. If you are acquainted with these principles, all of the rules begin to assume a logical pattern. Thus, much of the confusion is removed, and parliamentary procedure is made easier to understand and to apply.

The basic principles in outline are these:

1. *The Majority Rules.*

Perfect agreement is not always possible, although many church groups may prefer to avoid acting when a significant minority is in opposition and feelings run high. But in order to have some basis for decision in cases on which we cannot agree and must act, we adopt the principle that the desires of the majority will be carried out. This majority is defined as being more than half of those voting. Those who choose not to vote are considered to be equally divided, for and against.

2. *The Rights of the Minority Must Be Protected.*

Although the majority rules, it cannot be granted unlimited power. In other words, we do not believe in the dictatorship of the majority. Every individual has certain personal rights, regardless of whether he happens to be in the majority or the minority. These rights include the right of free speech, the right of the secret ballot, the right to nominate for office, the right to be informed of the business before the assembly and the effects of proposed actions, and the right of the protection of the bylaws (or constitution) and rules of order of the organization. Even absentees have rights, which must be protected.

3. *Business Must Be Accomplished.*

Church boards and organizations hold business meetings in order to take action. The group welcomes the free presentation of all the facts and viewpoints on any problem in open discussion, but that discussion cannot consume the entire meeting. The group should welcome the advocate who supports a given position by the persuasive presentation of all the arguments at her command. However, a business meeting should not be turned into a debate. In the long run, the rules of procedure must operate to bring an end to the discussion and argument and make a decision possible.

4. *Human Feelings Must Be Respected.*

No group exists as an entity apart from the men and women who constitute the group. Just as courtesy must temper all of our social relationships, so it must also govern our group-business activities. The Christian acts in lowliness of mind, each esteeming the other better than himself (Phil. 2:3).

5. *Procedures Must Be Orderly.*

Parliamentary rules are similar to traffic regulations. A red light may force you to stop at an intersection when you would much prefer to rush ahead, but the movement of traffic requires that some wait while others proceed. The alternative to order is chaos, and then everyone suffers. All have the right to assume that the rules will be clearly stated and properly respected throughout the business meeting. Taking one thing at a time is usually the most orderly procedure; deal with each item in turn before permitting something else to intervene.

6. *Each Individual Must Be Treated Justly.*

Rich or poor, wise or foolish, all are alike before God and before the law (James 2:4). Members are to be treated equally, and justice is rendered to each, even when an individual is absent from the meeting itself. All should be treated fairly and in good faith.

7. *Each Individual Has the Right to Know What Is Going On.*

Be sure that all can hear and understand. Welcome questions, but try to anticipate the problems that may be bothering the members. Explain clearly, or ask others for explanations. Time spent in promoting understanding is usually time well spent.

8. *Work for Consensus.*

The ideal group would make all its decisions unanimously. Christians share a common faith, obey one Lord, and act in love toward one another. Aiming for perfection, they seek to be of one mind (II Cor. 13:11). However, the real world being what it is, we often fall short of this goal. Perhaps the only church to approach it was that early company of believers in Jerusalem (Acts 4:32), and we wonder about possible hyperbole in the report! Still, bear in mind the principle that no action at all is sometimes preferable to a split vote and a divided group.

Certain parliamentary procedures may help to achieve consensus, and an effective Chair should know and utilize them.

a. Take time in reaching decisions. Let your

14

members know ahead of time the issues to be faced and the motions to be considered. Avoid acting under the pressure of deadlines.

b. Use the amendment procedure. Often the majority can reword a motion to attract minority support.

c. Defer action. Utilize quiet personal discussion, apart from the argument of a business meeting. Come back to the motion later.

d. Utilize committees. A smaller group may be in a better position to assemble the facts and recommend a course of action acceptable to all. We will discuss these procedures in later chapters.

Obviously, these eight basic principles will sometimes contradict. The rights of the minority may interfere with the rapid accomplishment of business or with the rule of the majority. The course of expedience may not always be the course of courtesy, order, or justice. One can imagine some supercomputer programmed to give the proper weight to each of these principles in all possible situations. Such a computer does not exist, of course. Rather, the rules of parliamentary procedure have developed over the years to accomplish the same purpose, to keep each of the eight principles in its proper place and proportion in every possible situation the group may face.

THE CHAIR
AS A PERSON

Anyone who desires to be effective as a Chair or group leader should remember that her personality as evidenced by her bearing in front of the group is much more important to her success than all of the rules she can learn. The individual who fumbles and hesitates in giving a right decision may make a worse Chair than the one who gives a wrong decision in a tone of firm authority. This fact, however, is not intended as an excuse for those officers who do not know the essentials of parliamentary procedure. Every workman should be familiar with the tools of his trade. The good workman not only knows his tools but becomes proficient in their use. So the effective Chair must pay careful attention to the manner in which she puts her knowledge into action when she leads a group.

1. *Preparing for a Meeting*

a. Keep yourself informed. Be in touch with the pastor and with the members of the church staff. Your position as Chair probably makes you an ex-officio member of all committees except the nominating committee. Take the time to attend these meetings as often as possible. Serve as a channel of communication from group to group so that problems of conflict and duplication do not arise. Anticipate plans and projects as they begin to take shape.

b. Make arrangements as to time and place. You do not have the authority to make changes in meeting times specified in the bylaws or determined by group action. However, you can check to be certain that the room has been reserved, that it will be large enough for the meeting, that sufficient chairs will be on hand, and that the heating or cooling will be adequate. Remember that a key must be available to open the room prior to meeting time. Don't forget that parking space should be available for those driving to the meeting.

c. Give some thought to social arrangements. Business meetings go more smoothly if people are at ease. Will you need name tags? What about refreshments? Who will brew the coffee? Will the food be served before, during, or after the business meeting itself? What about cups, plates, napkins? Have you appointed someone to help serve, someone to help with the cleanup?

d. Prepare a preliminary agenda. Consult the pastor, members of the church staff, committee heads, and anyone to be listed for a part in the meeting. Talk to your group's secretary and review the minutes of the previous meeting. Look ahead to the next chapter in this book dealing with the order of business, and list the items pertaining to your meeting. Be specific. A vague section for "committee reports" is not adequate. List the individual committees that will be reporting. If you know a committee will not be reporting, don't list it. If possible, specify the nature of the report and the name of the individual who will give it. Remember that this agenda is only preliminary and will not become official until it is accepted by vote of the group in the meeting itself.

e. Notify your members. Announcements from the pulpit or in the church paper are appropriate but not adequate. Mail copies of your agenda to all concerned. Enlist a group of assistants to help you make phone calls to remind the membership a day or two ahead of the meeting.

f. Remind your leadership. Anyone listed in your agenda as having a part in the meeting should receive a phone call from you a day or two ahead of time. Be certain there is no misunderstanding as to the part each individual is expected to take in the meeting. A final check on room reservations, room keys, and refreshment plans could also avoid embarrassing surprises.

g. Be a good host or hostess. Arrive early. Make sure the room is properly arranged to facilitate the meeting you have planned. Check heating, cooling, and ventilation. Distribute any materials the members will need. Help prepare the refreshments. Greet the members as they arrive.

2. *In the Business Meeting*

a. Be brief. Most people accept a business meeting as a necessary evil, about as welcome as the first squeak in a new automobile. They attend through a sense of duty, or they endure the meeting while waiting for the speaker, program, or refreshments that will keep the evening from being a total loss. If you would be a popular Chair, aim to keep the business meeting as short as possible.

b. Be a leader. Don't be afraid of being a dictator. As long as the group has the power to control you by appealing from your decisions, the meeting will be essentially democratic. Sound like a leader. Let every person in the room hear every word you say. It's better to shout than to have someone wondering what you're muttering about. Look like a leader. Dress carefully enough so that you can stand before the audience without worrying about how you look. Women, don't overdo the jewelry, particularly ear rings and bracelets that jingle or call attention to themselves. Men, don't rattle the keys or change in your pockets. Stand straight. Look each one squarely in the eye.

c. Speak with authority. Give your rulings immediately and without hesitation. If you are not certain of the proper answer to a parliamentary problem, immediately give the answer that seems best, expecting the members to appeal from any unjust decision. Don't flaunt your knowledge in the faces of your group members, but don't leave any doubt about that knowledge.

d. Stand above petty differences. Under ordinary circumstances, your only participation in discussion is to supply information not possessed by anyone else. As a rule, refuse to cast a vote unless your vote is in a secret ballot or is needed to make or to break a tie. Take particular care to avoid the criticism that you favor a certain viewpoint or a certain clique. Be fair.

e. Maintain an orderly meeting. Insist on proper respect for a member who has the floor. All remarks should be addressed to you as the Chair. Members do not address one another directly. One should never impugn the character or motives of another. Maintain the dignity of the assembly. Insist that your group follow the rules of parliamentary procedure. On the other hand, remember that it is always out of order for any of your members to use those rules to obstruct business.

f. To control others, control yourself. Hold your temper and your tongue. Remember the "soft answer that turneth away wrath." A sense of humor may often prove your best aid in keeping a situation under control.

g. Keep the assembly informed. Every member should know exactly what is before the group at all times. Be certain that everyone knows the effects of an "aye" and a "no" vote before each vote is taken. As each item of business is handled, remind the members of what they have concluded and inform them of the next matter for their consideration. Don't condemn ignorance. If a member makes a wrong motion, suggest the right one for him.

h. Be modest. Don't be a show-off. Just as a member must not use parliamentary procedure to obstruct matters, the Chair must not use parliamentary procedure as a means of demonstrating her superior intellect or training.

3. *In the Committee Meeting*

a. Be patient. You are not serving as Chair to convince the group that your way is right or to force the members to carry out your wishes. Let them talk matters over in their own way and at their own time. Let them come to their own decision. Remember that, although their decision may not be nearly as effective as the one you wanted, it has one supreme advantage over yours—it's the decision of the group.

b. Be interested. Try to make each individual feel that his contribution has been of the greatest importance to the thinking of the group. Let your very attitude serve as an encouragement to those who would otherwise be too shy to say anything. Be a good listener.

c. Be objective. Remember that no one should argue for his viewpoint in a good group discussion. The members of the group should be engaging in a process of sharing their opinions and viewpoints. Let your attitude be characteristic of the discussion procedure.

d. Seek to understand people. Try to recognize the types of persons and their motives present in your group. Credit each person with the best possible motive for his actions. Individuals almost always do the thing that seems right in their own eyes. Try to understand the background or training that has been responsible for that viewpoint. Never attribute an unworthy motive to anyone unless the evidence is overwhelming.

e. Be alert. Listen to all of the comments made. Try to detect the feelings and sentiments in the group that are not being overtly expressed.

f. Develop the ability to analyze. Discover the implications involved in each comment made or viewpoint expressed. Be aware of the apparently minor details of the various aspects of the discussion.

g. Develop the ability to synthesize. Think in terms of the general development of the pattern of the discussion. Be able to add together the various individual contributions in order to see their bearing upon that pattern. Be aware of the relationship between the discussion outline as the group is developing it and your own outline made in preparing for the discussion. Don't reject the group's outline, but try to synthesize the various ideas presented. When the discussion lags, take the opportunity to share that synthesis with your group in a brief summary.

h. Express your sense of humor. Discussions that become too serious tend to involve personalities and turn into arguments. The appropriate use of a sense of humor can frequently prevent this development. In fact, a sense of humor is one tool you can use in stopping an argument that has already started.

i. Be able to phrase and rephrase remarks. Use

this ability to ensure complete understanding on the part of all group members and to relate each contribution to the pattern of the discussion as a whole. When you hear an important contribution, rephrase it; then ask the member if you correctly understood what he intended to say.

j. Don't take advantage of your position as Chair. Remember that this position lends you a certain amount of authority for the duration of the meeting. Any opinions that you might express will carry that authority. Therefore, refuse to express your opinions as a general rule. If you seem to assume the responsibility for carrying on the discussion, the group may decide to give you the complete responsibility and refuse to contribute to the discussion at all. Keep the group members conscious that the responsibility for the discussion lies with them, not with the Chair.

4. *During the Program*

a. Maintain the importance of time. Get the program started on time. Do your best to hold the performers or speakers to their time limits. Always make some arrangement with these individuals ahead of time for some system for warning them that their time is about to expire. Then, if the performer lacks the courtesy to observe the warning, you will be free to interrupt the performance.

b. Focus attention on the performer or speaker.

There is nothing worse than a Chair who "steals the scene" from those on her program. Beware of the bored expression, the eyes focused on some other center of attention. Beware of movements that distract the attention of the audience.

c. Fill the role of the cordial host or hostess. Make the audience feel optimistic about the quality and length of the program. Make the performers feel appreciated, at ease, and at home. Try to let all of your actions exhibit a spirit of good fellowship.

d. Give direction to the program. Try to arrange the various parts of the program in some sort of order. In general, the program should move from light and humorous matters into more serious things. This same rule may be applied to individual parts of the program as well. If the group sings a number of songs, for instance, the lighter songs should come first, the more serious songs later.

e. Be a good business manager. Make definite arrangements with the speakers or performers about the honorarium and expense money that they are to receive. Check with the treasurer of your organization before making any commitments, to be certain that the money is available. Make no expenditures that have not been previously authorized by the organization. Check with the treasurer again after the program to be certain that the performers have been paid.

f. Don't forget the duties of courtesy. What about flowers or a corsage for the performers or for your chief assistants? Thank those who deserve to be thanked—and perhaps even some who don't! Welcome the visitors. Express the appreciation of the group to the performers or speakers. When the whole thing is over, a sincere expression of thanks in a little note mailed to those concerned is always a good idea.

5. *Introducing a Speaker or Performer*

One of the important functions of the Chair or group leader, which requires a combination of her best personal attributes and all of the skill and training that she can acquire, is introducing a speaker or performer. By observing a few simple rules, however, most group leaders can do a perfectly acceptable job.

An effective introduction involves three basic steps. First, get the attention of the audience. Second, transfer that attention to the speaker or performer or to the subject matter about to be considered. Third, give the audience to the speaker or performer.

a. Gain and direct your group's attention. Plan a first sentence that will attract favorable attention from your listeners. Then, direct that attention toward the speaker or the subject matter or both. If your people are already eager to hear this speaker, emphasize the importance of the subject. If the audience is already interested in the subject, emphasize the qualifications and authority of the speaker. Do all of this briefly. Then conclude with one final sentence that turns the attention of the audience away from you and over to the speaker or performer.

b. Utilize the factors of curiosity and respect. You can build the interest of the audience in the speaker and his subject by making the audience curious about them. For instance, most introductions leave the name of the speaker for the very last, building curiosity. You can also create interest by emphasizing the importance of the speaker or subject. Be careful, however, that you don't exaggerate, which can become self-defeating.

c. Make the introduction fit the speaker and the occasion. Use a serious introduction for an occasion of great importance or a speaker of great dignity. Use a lighter introduction for lighter subjects or for old friends. Don't make the mood of every introduction the same. Don't feel that every introduction must begin with a joke, although an appropriate humorous story may be an effective way to gain initial attention.

d. Don't steal the speaker's thunder or attempt to give his speech for him. Don't focus attention on yourself or on anything except the speaker and his subject. The purpose of the introduction is not to establish yourself as an expert in the subject matter or as equal to the speaker in status and authority. Focus on the speaker. Then get out of the way and let him give the speech.

e. Follow an orderly procedure. The three steps

we have mentioned suggest the common order. Begin with a striking statement, a bit of humor, or perhaps a quotation designed to catch the attention of the listeners. Tell a little about the speaker's background or perhaps about his subject, limiting yourself to those items that are absolutely necessary for the audience's appreciation. Finally, turn the audience over to the speaker by some such remark as, "Therefore, it is with much interest that we turn to hear Professor Rutherford Q. Jones. Professor Jones." As you say these last words, turn to him, showing that you share the eagerness of all the others to hear him speak. If it is customary in your group, you may lead the applause at this point.

f. Be brief, which is the most important rule of all for a successful introduction. It has been said that the perfect introduction is that frequently heard in the media for the President: "Ladies and Gentlemen: The President of the United States." These words call for attention. They furnish the one important fact about the speaker, that he is the President. They say all that needs to be said about the subject, for any subject discussed by the President must be of importance to the nation. Finally, these words turn the audience over to the speaker. Let this introduction serve as your model.

THE ORDER
OF BUSINESS

Most groups have a standard order of business followed in all meetings, and church organizations usually have no need to deviate from this basic pattern. Those who are absent or who must arrive late should be able to assume that the meeting will follow this usual order. The items below constitute the normal outline. However, you may wish to prepare a more detailed list, specifying the precise committees to report and the individual items of business to be considered. This list, called an **agenda,** may be developed in consultation with the pastor and/or with an executive committee.

Distributing a proposed agenda to all members a few days ahead of the meeting not only serves to protect latecomers and absentees, it provides time for the members to give each item some thought ahead of time. Critical matters may become the object of special prayers. The proposed agenda also acquaints everyone with the volume of business to be covered in the meeting and thus discourages unnecessary discussion or distractions that could prolong it. Recognize, however, that an agenda may not be imposed on the group but must be adopted by the group itself.

During these procedures, while others are speak-

ing for periods of time, the Chair should be seated.
The following order is recommended:

1. *The Call to Order*

The Chair attracts the attention of the members by rapping with the gavel and says:

"The meeting will please come to order."

We assume that this action takes place promptly at the announced time for the beginning of the meeting. Start your meetings late, and you will soon find that the members arrive late.

At this time the Chair has made a quick count of the members to determine if a **quorum** is present. *Quorum* is defined as the number of members needed to conduct official business, and the number is usually given in the bylaws of the organization. If no such number is specified, the quorum for a church board or committee would be a majority of its membership. For a congregational meeting, the quorum is usually lower, sometimes consisting of the number who actually attend a properly called and advertised meeting. That is, if all members have been given an announcement of the meeting, sufficiently in advance, the number attending the meeting, no matter how small the group, would constitute a quorum.

If a quorum is not present, the group is unable to take official action. Proceed with the items listed below, in the hope that latecomers will arrive to constitute a quorum. If not, the assembly could discuss the various items of business but could not act upon them.

2. *Opening Exercises*

The official meeting of any church group may begin with prayer or a devotional period that may include the singing of a hymn and/or the reading of a scripture passage. The Chair says,
"We will be led in prayer (or devotions) by . . . . "
This aspect of the meeting must be prepared ahead of time. Do not wait until the last minute to ask someone to offer the prayer, lead the singing, or play the piano. If the Chair has neglected this duty, she then has the responsibility of fulfilling these obligations herself!

3. *Roll Call*

If a roll call is desired, the Chair should say,
"The Secretary will please call the roll."
Sometimes the Chair adds:
"Members will answer to their names by . . . ," stating the particular report or device that the individual member will use in answering to his name in roll call. Perhaps a favorite scripture verse, a word of encouragement, or an item for thanksgiving would be appropriate here.

The roll call enables the Chair to be certain that a quorum is, indeed, present. However, be careful that the opening exercises and roll call do not take too much time, causing the meeting to run late. Keep the proposed agenda in mind. Many groups save the roll-call time by asking people to sign a roster or to check their names on a roll sheet.

4. *Adoption of the Agenda*

At this point the group should officially adopt the agenda that has been distributed previously. The Chair says,

"Does anyone wish to propose a change in the agenda?"

Notice that in raising this question, the Chair is assuming a motion to adopt the agenda. Any changes to the agenda are technically motions to amend it. These should properly be offered, second-ed, and adopted by majority vote, a procedure we will discuss in detail later on. After all of the proposed changes have been considered, the Chair says,

"All those in favor of adopting the agenda, say 'aye' (pronounced "eye"). Those opposed say 'no.' The motion is carried, and the agenda is adopted."

Note that the Chair does not ask those opposed to give the "same sign." The expression "aye" means assent or agreement. Those who disagree should be asked to say "no."

In place of this formal vote, the Chair may use the

"general consent" procedure, in effect asking for a unanimous vote, a procedure that also will be discussed later.

At this point in the meeting the agenda may be changed and finally adopted by simple majority votes. Once it has been adopted, however, it becomes the official guide for the meeting. It subsequently requires a two-thirds vote to change it.

The agenda may be as detailed as the group wishes to make it. As a rule, however, one should avoid specifying time limits on any of the items or including a time schedule in the agenda. Such a time schedule, adopted at this point, would become official and would unnecessarily restrict the allotment of time as the meeting progresses. The time spent on each item may better be handled by other procedures later on.

5. *The Reading of the Minutes of the Last Meeting*

The Chair says,
"The Secretary will read the minutes of the last meeting."

After the minutes have been read, the Chair stands once more and asks,
"Are there any corrections of the minutes?"

If no corrections are offered, the Chair states,
"The minutes stand approved as read."

If corrections are offered, the Secretary is instructed to make the necessary changes. If members disagree as to what was done, a majority vote should determine the matter. Finally, the Chair states,

"The minutes stand approved as corrected."

A group should never "dispense with" the reading of the minutes in the sense of avoiding them entirely. There must always be the opportunity for members to examine this record and make corrections where necessary. The reading may be deferred until a later time for some reason.

Some groups circulate printed copies of the minutes in advance of the meeting, in which case it would not be necessary for the secretary to read every word for approval. In such a case, if no one suggests changes, the Chair says,

"The minutes stand approved as distributed."

6. *Correspondence*

The Chair says,

"Has there been any correspondence since the last meeting?"

The Secretary then reads any letters that do not require action by the group. Lengthy letters may be summarized. Correspondence which requires action should be read later, during "New Business."

7. *The Pastor's Report*

At this time the Chair may call on the pastor for whatever report he or she may wish to make. The reports of other members of the church staff may follow. In each case, the Chair should ask for any questions. The assumption here is that these reports are for information only. The pastor would probably submit items requiring action to the appropriate committees to be included in the committee report, later. If he does make a recommendation directly to the group at this point, however, he should not move the adoption of this recommendation. Another member should perform this function. The group should proceed to discuss and to act upon this recommendation immediately.

8. *The Chair's Report*

The Chair may report items of general information at this time. Again, items requiring action may come through the appropriate committees, or a member may move the adoption of a recommendation made at this time by the Chair. Other officers may also report in the same manner.

9. *The Treasurer's Report*

The Chair says,
"Will the treasurer please read the financial report."
When the reading is finished, the Chair asks:
"Are there any questions? (Pause) If none, the treasurer's report will be filed, subject to audit."

Notice that no action is taken in response to a treasurer's report. The group never votes to approve or to accept this report. No voting procedure could possibly add or delete a penny from the funds in the treasury anyway. Each year the treasurer's accounts should be audited. When the report of the auditing committee is adopted at that time, it serves to approve the treasurer's records.

10. *Committee Reports*

The Chair calls on each committee chair in turn for a report. Permanent (standing) committees should report ahead of temporary (special or ad hoc) committees. For detailed instructions on handling these reports, see the section of this handbook dealing with committees. Remember, however, that reports containing information only do not require action on the part of the group. Limit the group action to committee recommendations.

11. *Unfinished Business*

The Chair proceeds to each item of unfinished business as listed in the agenda, previously adopted. These matters, left over from the previous meeting, are discussed and voted in the order in which they appear on the agenda. Notice that the proper expression is "unfinished" business, not "old" business.

12. *New Business*

The Chair says,
"We will now consider any new business."
As a rule, the Chair should avoid allowing the group to discuss some subject before any motion is made. Such discussions should be held in committee meetings. The group as a whole would do well to limit itself to hearing motions, putting them into the proper shape, and taking action upon them.

13. *Program*

Once new business has been completed, the Chair should introduce the head of the program committee or the individual in charge of whatever program (if any) has been planned. The Chair and secretary would naturally sit in the audience for the duration of this program.

14. *Closing Matters*

When the program is completed, the Chair resumes the leadership of the meeting. He would then make some fitting remark about the program or the speaker. Then at this time the Chair or other members may give any closing announcements. A closing prayer or benediction would be appropriate here.

15. *Adjournment*

If everything has obviously been completed at this point, the Chair may simply say,

"The meeting is adjourned."

However, some member may also say,

"I move that we adjourn." Such a motion should be handled in much the same manner as other motions. Ordinarily, it would not be discussed. The Chair would get a second to the motion, put it to a vote, and announce the result:

"The motion is adopted. The meeting is adjourned."

Once again, in this situation the Chair could use the "general consent" procedure to good advantage.

Some groups may prefer to have the closing prayer or benediction at this point. Whatever your practice, be sure you have made prior arrangements. It is not courteous to ask any individual, even the pastor, to offer a prayer without advance notice.

HANDLING A MOTION

Christian groups may come together for many reasons, social, educational, inspirational, or whatever. Scriptures remind us that we are not to neglect attendance at such meetings (Heb. 10:25). But the particular meetings addressed in this handbook are those called for the purpose of conducting business. In such meetings the group forms policy, specifies its positions, takes action, and generally carries out whatever work it thinks appropriate to its nature and purposes. However, no organization possesses a group mind that invents such courses of action. All such ideas originate in the thought processes of individuals.

Thus every democratic organization needs some sort of machinery that will take an idea from the mind of an individual, examine it, refine it, and finally turn it into the official position or policy of the group, a policy on which the group as a whole will act. This machinery is the **main motion** in a business meeting, and the proper handling of a motion is one of the major challenges to the abilities of the man or woman serving as Chair.

The steps detailed below are those used in handling an ordinary "main" motion. Certain special types of motions vary from this procedure in one way or another. These motions will be considered in detail later on. Both the Chair and each member should be very careful to use the exact statements given. Mistakes in this regard are very common, disturbing, and can be seriously detrimental to the democratic functioning of the group. For further discussion, see *RONR*, pp. 31-56, the section titled "The Handling of a Motion."

1. *The Member Obtains the Floor*.

That is, one asks the Chair for the undivided attention of the group. The member does this by rising (unless the group is very small) and addressing the Chair, saying,

"*Mr. Chairman!*"

The assumption here is that the Chair is male. If a woman is presiding, the traditional address would be "Madam Chairman." The expression "Madam Chairperson" is sometimes heard but is very awkward. Some may prefer to use the procedure of this book and say, "Mr. Chair" or "Madam Chair."

Small groups often follow the practice of having the member remain seated, perhaps raising a hand in addressing the Chair. But since asking for the floor also indicates the intention of speaking, the member should rise if the group is large enough that speakers normally stand to be seen and heard.

2. *The Chair Recognizes the Member*.

The Chair usually addresses the member by name: "*Mrs. Jones*."

Other forms of recognition are also possible, with the Chair perhaps nodding in the direction of the member if the group is small. In any event, the member may not speak until she has been recognized in some way by the Chair. Then she is considered to "have the floor," the right to address the assembly. Throughout this book, the reference to "gaining the floor" or "having the floor" will mean that a member has properly addressed the Chair and been recognized.

3. *The Member States the Motion.*

"*I move that we. . . .*"

The expression "I make a motion that. . . ." is not quite proper and should be avoided. The member should speak clearly and distinctly so that all may hear and understand. The motion should be as complete as possible so that no unnecessary changes need be made. Long motions should be submitted to the Chair in writing.

4. *The Motion Is Seconded.*

A member does not need to rise, address the Chair, or be recognized in order to second a motion. He only needs to call,

"*Second!*" or

"*I second the motion!*"

The second does not necessarily indicate approval

of a motion, and the one who seconds it may ultimately vote against it. The principle involved is that the group should not waste time on ideas of interest to only one member. The second demonstrates that at least one additional person believes the motion is worth some discussion, some attention by the group as a whole.

In cases where the motion clearly has the support of more than one person (as, for example, a motion that originates from a committee), this step may be omitted. An action taken by the group is never invalidated on the basis that the motion was not seconded.

If no second is offered, the Chair should ask, *"Is the motion seconded?"*

It is not correct to ask, "Do I hear a second?" No one knows what the Chair can hear. If no one then offers to second the motion, the Chair states, *"Since there is no second, the motion is not before this meeting."*

5. *The Chair States the Motion.*

Once the second has been offered, the Chair repeats the motion that the member offered, saying, *"It has been moved and seconded that we . . . ."*

This step is particularly important, not only because it ensures that all are informed of the motion to be discussed but also because it marks a change in the ownership of the motion. Up until this point, the motion belongs to the member who is offering it. She may change it or rephrase it in any way she likes. The member seconding has no control, although he may withdraw his second if he objects to some change.

But once the motion has been stated by the Chair, it belongs to the entire group. No changes may be made in the motion without the permission of the majority of the group, even if those changes are recommended by the one making the motion or the one who seconded it. Neither the motion nor its second can be withdrawn without majority permission, as indicated by some sort of vote. Any member objecting to a change may force the group to go through the amendment procedure, requiring one of the special motions that we will discuss later.

6. *The Chair Calls for Discussion.*

After stating the motion, the Chair asks, *"Is there any discussion?"*

An older form of this question was "Are you ready for the question?" This form, however, may be understood as an implication that discussion is not wanted, and therefore it should be avoided. The Chair's obligation at this point is to encourage a full discussion of the question at hand.

7. *The Members Discuss the Motion.*

Notice the following guidelines for this period.
a. Each member who wishes to speak must first

obtain the floor, addressing the Chair and being recognized, just as if he had a new motion to offer.

b. The Chair offers no opinions on the motion. His job is to keep order. Upon occasion he may supply needed information about the subject if he, because of his office, has knowledge not possessed by the group, but he should not become involved in the argument.

c. Discussion must be confined to the last motion placed before the group, in this case the main motion that is being considered.

d. Speakers should avoid personality conflicts and not attribute improper motives to other members. Even the use of the name of another member should be avoided by using such designations as "the previous speaker," etc. All remarks should be directed to the Chair, by making statements such as,

"Madam Chair, the previous speaker stated that . . . , but I feel that . . . ."

e. Ordinarily, the one who made the motion is given the first opportunity to discuss it.

f. Other things being equal, the one who rises and addresses the Chair first is assigned the floor. If anyone rises so soon as to interrupt the previous speaker, he is out of order and may not be given the floor.

g. If many people desire to speak, the Chair tries to alternate the floor, recognizing first one in favor of the motion, then one opposed to the motion. To facilitate this procedure, the Chair may ask an individual if she intends to speak for or against the motion before the Chair grants her recognition.

h. A member who has spoken once on a motion should not be allowed to speak a second time until all members who desire to express themselves for the first time have done so.

i. Strict obedience to the rules in *RONR* would limit all members to two speeches on any one motion and would limit any one speech to ten minutes. However, speeches in a modern business meeting are rarely more than a minute or two in length. The flow of the argument often requires more than two brief comments from the chief spokespersons for either side. The wisest course for the modern Chair is to permit as many brief speeches as the discussion requires, only setting limits when speakers begin to repeat what was said earlier.

j. The chief objective of the Chair in this period is to insure the freedom of speech. The proper method for cutting short the debate will be discussed later. At this point, the Chair should act so that all wishing to speak may be heard. Watch out for the impatient member who rudely calls "Question! Question!" without obtaining the floor and perhaps even interrupting another speaker. Such members should be called to order and silenced so that the speaker may continue.

8. *The Chair Determines that Discussion Is Finished.*

When members stop rising to claim the floor to discuss the motion, the Chair asks,

"Is there any further discussion?"

Again, the old form "Are you ready for the question?" is sometimes heard but should be avoided. If further discussion is offered, the Chair waits until no one is claiming the floor and then repeats,

"Is there any further discussion?"

When this question no longer brings out any discussion, the Chair immediately proceeds to the next step.

9. *The Chair Restates the Motion.*

The Chair says,

"If there is no further discussion, we are ready to vote. The question is on the motion to . . . ." (Here the complete motion is repeated). Do not omit this step, assuming that the members surely know the motion by this time. All need to be reminded of the precise wording of the motion.

10. *The Members Vote on the Motion.*

The Chair says,

"All those in favor of the motion say 'aye.' Those opposed say 'no.'"

In each case, the Chair makes clear to the members what they are to do to express their votes. Any meeting may involve several methods of expressing a vote. Common methods are:

a. Viva Voce (by voice). This procedure is the one outlined above. In place of calling for the "aye" and "no" votes, the Chair may call for a show of hands.

b. Rising. The members for and against a motion are asked to stand. This method should always be used if the motion requires a two-thirds vote, since it enables the Chair to count the vote. (In a very small group, a show of hands may be a reasonable alternative to the rising vote.) If the Chair has not used this method, and the result of the viva voce vote is in doubt, any member may force a rising vote by calling,

"Division!"

or

"I call for a division of the house!"

This request is similar to a "second" in that the member need not go through the formality of addressing the Chair and gaining the floor. The request forces the Chair to take a rising vote, although it does not, technically, force a counted vote. The Chair simply repeats the voting, this time asking those who favor the motion to rise. The rules do not require the Chair to count those standing. However, the Chair would always be wise to count the affirmative votes while these members are up. The negative vote, then, may or may not be counted, depending on how close the vote seems to be.

c. Ballot. The members vote by marking slips of paper. This method is very time-consuming, so it is rarely used except in elections or in those cases where the bylaws of the organization require a ballot vote. In any particular case, however, the members may decide, by majority vote, that they want a particular vote taken by ballot.

d. Roll Call. The Secretary calls the membership roll, and each member responds with "aye," "no," or "abstain." This method is also time consuming, but it stands in contrast to the ballot since it puts each member on record. It is usually limited to representative groups in which each member is responsible to a constituency that has the right to know how its representative voted.

e. General consent. The Chair states,

"If there is no objection, we will . . ." (stating the action that the motion requires).

The Chair should then pause to allow for objections to be made. If no objections are offered, the motion is considered to be passed by unanimous vote. To make this situation clear, the Chair should add,

"It is a vote. We will . . . ."

If anyone objects, the vote must then be taken by one of the other methods. This method of general consent is very useful when the entire group agrees that certain things should be done and the Chair wants to speed the procedure.

The Chair, as a member of the group, has the right to vote if she pleases. Ordinarily, she will refuse to reveal her opinions, not voting unless the vote is by ballot. However, if her vote will either create or break a tie, she will probably want to use it. In any case, the motion is lost on a tie vote. An ordinary motion requires a majority vote to pass, and a majority is one more than half of the votes cast. For example, when voting to create a tie, the Chair would make the following announcement:

"The count of the vote indicates 50 in favor and 49 against. However, the Chair votes 'no.' The count is thus 50 to 50, and the motion fails, since it lacks a majority."

When breaking a tie, the Chair would say,

"The count of the vote indicates 50 in favor and 50 against. However, the Chair votes 'aye.' The count is thus 51 to 50, and the motion passes."

If the vote is by secret ballot, the Chair casts her ballot along with the rest. In such a case she would not get a second vote. If the ballot count ends in a tie, the motion fails.

The matter of abstentions in voting is frequently misunderstood. When a vote is taken, each member has three alternatives. She may vote "aye," "no," or may abstain from voting. The abstentions have no effect on the outcome of the vote, since they are assumed to be equally divided for and against the motion. Thus a roll call vote may reveal 5 voting "aye," 4 voting "no," and 100 abstaining from voting. In this case, the motion would pass by a vote of 5 to 4. Usually, the abstentions are not even counted unless there could be some question about the presence of a quorum at the time the vote was taken.

11. *The Chair Announces the Result of the Vote.*

This announcement should include the following four items of information:

a. The outcome of the vote. If there was no doubt about the result, the Chair says,

"The aye's have it."

If there was some question about which side had the majority, the Chair says,

"The aye's seem to have it." (Pause) *"The aye's have it."*

The pause is to allow for any calls for a rising vote (a division of the house) that might be offered.

b. The status of the motion. The Chair says,

"The motion is carried," or *"The motion is lost."*

c. The effect of this vote. The Chair adds,

"We will therefore . . ." (stating the action which the motion requires the organization to take).

d. The next immediately pending business. In this case we have finished handling an original main motion, an item of new business. The Chair would thus add,

"Is there any further business to come before us?"

If the vote has just concluded an item of unfinished business, the Chair will naturally announce the next item on the agenda at this point.

HANDLING
SUBSIDIARY MOTIONS

The procedure outlined in the previous chapter takes an idea from the mind of one member and makes it the policy of the total group. However, the procedure does not always go as smoothly as indicated, and with good reason. We have assumed a perfect motion that needs no revision. We have confronted the individuals in the group with three alternatives in regard to that motion—to vote in favor, to vote against, or to abstain from voting. Few ideas come before business meetings in such perfect form, so a democratic group offers its members additional alternatives.

A group member has the following options when she first hears a new motion offered to the group:

a. I can't favor that idea, but I would like to bury it quietly, without a direct vote.

b. The idea has possibilities, but some changes need to be made in the motion.

c. The idea needs further study; a small group of us should look into it.

d. We are not yet ready to act on that idea; we should put it off.

e. Almost all of us favor (or oppose) that idea, and further talk about it is a waste of time.

Any or all of these possibilities might occur to a

member once the original motion is placed before the group. Each member should have the right to share this reaction with the other members and, if enough of them agree, to treat the main motion according to this preference. To accomplish this end, *RONR* permits a series of **subsidiary motions** that may be applied to the main motion before it is voted.

At this point, then, you should think of two classes of motions. First, there are **main motions** that accomplish the business of the organization. Then there are **subsidiary motions** that are used to modify, refine, or affect the main motion in some way. Perhaps you have heard the saying that a group cannot have two motions in front of it at the same time. In keeping with our principle of orderly procedure, this saying is correct insofar as main motions are concerned. However, while a main motion is pending before the group, members may offer a number of subsidiary motions. Each subsidiary motion must be handled in turn and voted before the main motion finally comes to a vote. A more complete discussion will be found in *RONR*, pp. 123-207, "Subsidiary Motions."

The procedure of handling a subsidiary motion differs in some respects from that of handling a main motion. The well-informed Chair should be able to answer the following questions about each motion that he hears, in order to dispose of that motion properly and with due consideration of the basic principles that we outlined earlier:

    a. What type of motion is it?

    b. What motions may it displace in receiving the

attention of the group, and what motions may displace it?

c. Does it require a second?

d. May it be discussed?

e. May it be changed or amended in any way?

f. What vote does it require, majority or two-thirds?

g. What will be the effects of passing this motion? As stated earlier, five possibilities may occur to the group as it considers a main motion. These give rise to five subsidiary motions. You may think of these as being more powerful than the main motion, since a subsidiary motion may displace the main motion for the time being and be handled first. As *RONR* puts it, subsidiary motions take precedence (pronounced "pre-**seed**-ens") over a main motion.

Subsidiary motions also have an order of precedence among themselves. Give careful attention, then, to the order in which we discuss these subsidiary motions. We begin with the weakest of them, one that barely has the power to displace a main motion, and we proceed toward the more powerful ones that not only take precedence over main motions but also over other subsidiary motions.

1. *The Motion to Postpone the Main Motion Indefinitely*

The purpose of this motion is to bury the main motion quietly, without a direct vote. In other words, the motion that is postponed indefinitely never comes before the group for a vote; this subsidiary motion kills it.

Sometimes the opponents of the main motion also use this subsidiary motion as a parliamentary maneuver to gain a test vote on the main motion. That is, they move to postpone the main motion indefinitely. If the motion passes, the main motion has been defeated without a vote, which is their objective. If the motion to postpone indefinitely fails, then the main motion remains before the group for discussion and vote, and other steps may still be taken to defeat it.

To make this motion, a member gains the floor and says,

"I move that we postpone this motion indefinitely."

At least, that is what the member would say, if all were familiar with *RONR*. Such, unfortunately, is frequently not the case. Therefore, often the member will say,

"I move that we lay this matter on the table" or *"I move that we table this matter."*

The motion requires a second. It is debatable, and the discussion may go into all the merits and shortcomings of the main motion, since the effect would be to kill the main motion. This motion cannot be amended or changed in any way, since it presents the group with only two alternatives: to kill the main motion or to let it remain. It requires a simple majority vote to pass. If it passes, the main motion to which it applies is dead, and the Chair should move to the next item on the agenda.

Do not confuse this motion with another, the motion to table, which will be discussed later. One usually hears "I move we table it," when the intent is to kill the main motion. The Chair should determine the intent of the member. If the intent was to kill the main motion, the Chair should treat this subsidiary motion as one to postpone indefinitely, calling for discussion. (The actual motion to lay a matter on the table is intended to defer action under emergency conditions and is not debatable.)

2. *The Motion to Amend the Main Motion*

When the group does not like the wording of the main motion, it may change that wording to suit the members by amending it. They may add words, remove words, or substitute one thing for another. (They may not accomplish two of these aims in the same amendment, however.) The mover of the main motion does not necessarily need to approve the amendment. When the vote is taken on the amendment and it passes, the motion itself is still not passed. The amendment only changes the wording of the main motion, and the vote on the main motion must still take place.

Amendments may be stated in many ways. One would be for the member to rise, address the Chair, and say,

"I move that we amend the motion by adding (striking,

substituting) the words . . . after the words . . . , so that the motion will read . . . ."

The wording of the amendment itself may not be desired by the group, so that a second amendment might be offered to change the wording of the first amendment. The amendment to the main motion may then be called a "primary" amendment and the amendment to the amendment a "secondary" amendment. The process may not be carried any further than that, however; "tertiary" amendments are not permitted, since they would make the whole procedure too complex and confusing.

Amendments must be seconded. They may be discussed, but the discussion is limited to the amendment itself and may not go into other aspects of the main motion until the amendment is decided. Amendments are handled one at a time. An amendment to change another portion of the main motion is not permitted until the amendment before the group is decided, one way or the other. A majority vote is adequate to pass the amendment and make the desired change in the wording of the main motion.

The amendment must be germane to the main motion; that is, it must deal with the same subject matter as the main motion. A "rider" in the congressional sense, an amendment that introduces a new subject, is not permitted in an ordinary business meeting.

However, the amendment need not be in harmony with the original motion. In fact, it may make changes in wording so radical that the intent of the original motion is completely frustrated. The only limits are that the amendment must not simply reverse the vote on the original motion. That is, if the original motion calls for the expenditure of a sum of money, an amendment would be out of order which simply introduces the word "not"—that we not expend that sum of money. This objective could be gained by simply voting "no" on the original motion.

One sometimes hears the expression "friendly amendment." It simply means an amendment that the author feels will be accepted by the mover of the original main motion. Upon hearing such an amendment, the Chair may save time by calling for approval by general consent. If anyone objects, however, the standard procedure must be followed, with discussion and a vote.

Remember that the original main motion has been stated by the Chair and belongs to the group as a whole. No single individual, not even the one who offered the motion in the first place, may change its wording without the consent of the group as a whole, given by means of a vote of some sort, often by general consent.

In some cases a member may offer a substitute motion as an amendment. This simply means that the member wishes to replace the entire main motion with another one of different wording. Naturally, the proposed substitute must be germane to the original motion. When a substitute is offered, the Chair uses the following procedure:

a. The original main motion is open for discussion and secondary amendments.

b. The proposed substitute is open for discussion (which may also involve the merits of the original wording) and secondary amendments.

c. The question of the substitution is put to a vote:

"All those in favor of substituting motion B for motion A indicate by saying 'aye.' "

At this point the group actually has two motions before it. One is the original main motion (motion A), which has been discussed and which may have been reworded by the amendment process. The second is the "substitute" motion (motion B), which also has been discussed and may have been amended. Technically, motion B is itself a primary amendment, proposed as a substitute for motion A. Now the group must decide which of these two motions is to remain before it. Shall motion B replace motion A on the floor for group consideration? Notice once again that we are dealing with the wording of motions— shall motion A be reworded so that it becomes motion B? The vote here does not adopt either motion.

d. The remaining motion, either A or B, is then open for further discussion and amendment.

e. This remaining motion is then put to a vote and adopted or rejected.

The amendment process is extremely important for church groups that value consensus. Sometimes a slight change in a word or a phrase may transform a highly controversial motion into one that receives unanimous support. You may wish to consult the detailed discussion found in *RONR*, pp. 127-64.

3. *The Motion to Refer the Main Motion to a Committee*

When the group as a whole does not have the time or the information to decide on the matter, it may wish to allow some existing or "standing" committee to handle it or to create a new special committee to handle it for them. To be complete, the motion that sends the matter to committee should include the following information: To what committee? How many members? How appointed? What instructions or power will the committee have? When should the committee report on the matter? If the motion to refer to committee lacks some of this information, the Chair should have the member add it to her motion before it is stated for the assembly.

If the motion is passed without some of this essential information, the Chair should ask the assembly to decide these questions before going on to other matters. The Chair does not have the power arbitrarily to fill in these details himself. He asks for suggestions from the group and then takes a vote on each suggestion until one receives a majority vote. A complete form of this motion might be as follows: The member gains the floor and says,

"I move that we refer this matter to our finance committee to investigate the effects of the proposed

expenditure on our budget and report to us at our next meeting."

This motion would require a second. Discussion is permitted, but the discussion would be limited to various issues in connection with the committee action. Should we let the committee handle it? Is the finance committee the proper group? Does a report to our next meeting give the committee adequate time? The discussion should not go into the merits of the main question at this point.

Amendments to the motion to refer to committee are also possible. One might move to strike "finance committee" and insert "a special task force of three to be appointed by the Chair," for example. A majority vote passes the motion, and the main motion is referred to the specified committee. This committee then has control over the main motion until it give its report or until the assembly takes further action to remove the matter from its control.

4. The Motion to Postpone the Main Motion to a Certain Time

This motion postpones action on the matter. As described in *RONR*, it always specifies the time limit of the postponement. Ordinarily, when that time limit has expired, the original matter will again come before the group. Thus the member says,

"I move that we postpone consideration of this matter

until our next meeting," or *"I move that we postpone consideration of this matter for ten minutes."*

This motion requires a second and is open for discussion of the merits of the postponement and the time limit set. Amendments in regard to the time are acceptable. A majority vote passes the motion. The member may not postpone a motion beyond the next meeting, since this would deprive those present at the next meeting of the right to consider the matter. That is, if a motion were postponed from meeting one to meeting three, the members in meeting two would have to override what was done in order to take up that matter early, in meeting two instead of meeting three. Such action would infringe on the rights of absentees, who would be assuming that the item would not be discussed until meeting three. To avoid such difficulties, motions cannot be postponed beyond the next meeting. Items postponed until the next meeting would come up under "unfinished business" in that meeting. At that point, a given motion could be postponed again, if the members are not yet ready to act.

Some parliamentary authorities would permit a motion to postpone the main question with no time limit specified. The present writer sees nothing wrong with the assembly adopting such a postponement, provided that the members are aware of the mechanism needed to bring the main question once again to the floor. This mechanism will be discussed later under the heading "Some Special Main Motions." The motion to take a matter from the table

would be used for this purpose, using the form,
*"I move that we resume consideration of the motion
to . . . ."*

5. *The Motion to Limit Discussion, or the Motion to Put an End to Discussion*

The purpose of these motions is to limit or stop the discussion of the motion before the group, thus forcing the group to vote on the matter. However, since these motions violate the basic right of free speech, they may only be passed by a two-thirds affirmative vote of those voting. The proper way to make the motion to limit discussion is to address the Chair, be recognized, and say,

"I move that we limit the discussion of this motion to five minutes," or *"I move that we limit the discussion to one speech for and one against the motion."*

Such a motion would require a second and would not be open to discussion, since its purpose is to reduce the talk and proceed to a vote. Either motion could be amended in regard to the limit proposed. An amendment might be offered to the first motion, to change five minutes to read "two minutes," for example. Or the second motion might be amended to read "two speeches for and two against the motion." Such an amendment could not be discussed and would require a majority vote, since its only purpose is to reword the original motion limiting discussion.

The action on the final motion to limit the discussion would take a two-thirds vote.

A member may also move to end the discussion entirely. In this instance, he would address the Chair, be recognized, and then say,

"I move that we end the discussion and take a vote."

This motion would also require a second and a two-thirds vote to pass. It could not be amended, since only two alternatives are possible: to stop the discussion or to continue it.

This motion is often expressed in other ways. For example, a member may move to vote immediately. One other phrasing of this motion, actually recommended by *RONR*, is especially confusing. A member who happens to know this outmoded procedure may address the Chair and say,

"I move the previous question."

Don't be misled. The member simply wants the discussion ended. If there is a second to this motion, rephrase it so your people will understand, saying,

"It has been moved and seconded to end the discussion and proceed to an immediate vote on our motion. All those in favor of ending the discussion please rise. Be seated. Those opposed to ending the discussion please rise. Be seated."

However the idea is expressed, if the member intends to proceed to an immediate vote without further discussion, rephrase his motion, as indicated above, so all the members will understand the matter they are being asked to decide. When the vote has been counted, the Chair would announce the result of the vote. If two-thirds favor this motion, his announcement would consist of the usual four items:

a. *"The vote is thirty yes and fifteen no."*

b. *"The motion passes by the necessary two-thirds."*

c. *"We will immediately proceed to a vote on the main motion."*

d. *"We are now voting on the motion to . . .* (repeating the motion). *All those in favor, indicate by saying 'aye.' Those opposed say 'no'."*

One should be very cautious about using these motions to limit or end discussion, particularly in a church organization. Free speech is a basic right, and restrictions upon it should not be taken lightly. Furthermore, additional discussion may help to bring about a consensus, the ideal in the consideration of any motion.

Never accept a motion to end the discussion before any discussion has taken place. Even a two-thirds majority should not be permitted to stifle discussion entirely.

Remember that cries of "Question! Question!" from your group do not constitute official motions. A member must rise, address the Chair, and be granted the privilege of speaking in order to move to end discussion. Shouting "Question," particularly if it interrupts a speaker, is very rude, and the member who does it should be called to order.

Don't be frightened by the mathematics of the two-thirds vote, even if you had problems with arithmetic in grammar school. Pay no attention to those who abstain from voting. When you count the votes, simply double the "no" vote. If the "yes" vote is equal to or greater than the "no" vote doubled, you have the necessary two-thirds.

Since one subsidiary motion may be tacked onto another, a group could have a whole series of motions before it at once. Suppose, for example, that when a main motion is pending, a subsidiary motion is first offered to amend it. Then, while the amendment is being discussed, someone moves to send the whole thing to a committee. Then a fourth member moves to postpone the matter until the next meeting. At this point a motion to end the discussion on all of the pending motions would be in order. A member could address the Chair, gain the floor, and say,

"I move that we end the discussion on all matters pending."

This motion would be handled like any other motion to end debate. It requires a second, cannot itself be discussed, and is passed by a two-thirds vote. If it passes, the Chair would take an immediate vote on each of the pending motions in turn—postpone, then (if this fails)—refer to a committee, then (if this fails)—amend, then—the main motion. Remember that this move also cuts off any further proposals to amend the main motion.

As you think of all these subsidiary motions, remember that they have an order of precedence within themselves. They increase in power in the order in which we have discussed them. The motion to postpone indefinitely is the weakest of the lot and is only in order when the main motion is being discussed. Amendments are more powerful. Thus an amendment may be offered to a motion when the motion to postpone it indefinitely is before the group. A motion to refer the whole matter to a committee would be in order when an amendment is being discussed. However, a motion to refer the matter to a committee would not be in order when the motion to postpone the whole thing until the next meeting is before the group. Finally, motions in regard to ending or limiting discussion are the most powerful of all and would be in order when any one of the other subsidiary motions is being discussed.

HANDLING
INCIDENTAL MOTIONS

By using the **subsidiary motions,** a group should be able to take the original main motion, the idea of one of its members or committees, improve it, get it into the best possible form, and then adopt it as the policy or action of the entire group. However, that process may not go smoothly. Certain situations may arise from the group process itself that require the attention of the membership. A number of incidental motions exist to deal with these problems of group function as they arise.

You could think of these various classes of motions as similar to driving an automobile through traffic. The **main motion** is like the original path of the automobile from point of origin to the driver's destination. **Subsidiary motions** resemble the various traffic controls along the way—the red lights, yield signs, or detours. Incidental motions pertain to the traffic control machinery itself—the electricity supplying the traffic lights, or the highway patrolmen enforcing the laws.

In similar fashion, incidental motions assure efficient group function. The list below is not complete, and you may need to refer to *RONR* for the unusual ones. (The section on "Incidental Motions" will be found on pp. 247-93. But see also the section on "Lay on the Table," pp. 207-16, and the discussion of the "Question of Privilege," pp. 223-29.)

This chapter describes the motions you are most likely to need.

1. *The Motion to Lay a Matter on the Table, or to Postpone It Temporarily*

This motion is rarely needed and should be saved for emergency situations only. Groups use it in cases of conflict on matters demanding their attention. Perhaps a program follows the business meeting, and the speaker for the program operates under time constraints due to another engagement or an airline schedule. The last motion before the group is requiring more time than anyone anticipated, and the program ought to begin. That motion could be laid on the table; then, following the departure of the speaker, the motion could be taken up again. Or another possibility may be that item 12 on the agenda is being discussed profitably and at length, but item 13 demands immediate action. In this case, item 12 could be laid on the table and then taken up again after item 13 has been handled.

The procedure is as follows: A member gains the floor and says,

"I move that we lay this matter on the table," or *"I move that we table this matter."*

The motion requires a second and is put to an immediate vote, with no discussion. A simple majority passes it. Once it is passed, the motion or group of motions to which it applies would be put aside until the group passes another motion to take it (or them) from the table, a motion that we will discuss later as a special type of main motion.

The motion to table never has a time limit attached to it. Since it confronts the group with only two alternatives, to defer or not to defer action on pending matters, no amendment is possible.

If the group wishes to defer action for a specified period of time, the proper motion would be the one to postpone, discussed earlier as the fourth of the subsidiary motions. Notice that these two motions are quite different in their purpose and orientation. The motion to postpone to a specific time is subsidiary to the main motion. Its purpose is to delay action on that main motion for a period of time. The motion to lay the matter on the table, however, is incidental to the situation and really has little to do with acting on the main motion. It means that some emergency has arisen in the meeting, and the main motion must be put aside to handle that emergency.

You will notice that the motion "to lay a matter on the table" may be used in two very different ways, asking the group to do different things under two very different circumstances.

a. In the first instance, the member moving to table really wants to kill the main motion. Under these circumstances, the motion to table is a subsidiary motion. It is debatable. It is also the weakest of the subsidiary motions, and it cannot be entertained when any other subsidiary motion is pending.

b. In the second case, however, the member moving to table wants to defer action on the main motion due to some emergency situation that has arisen. Under these circumstances, the motion to table would be classed as an incidental motion, incidental to the situation that has arisen. It is not debatable. As an incidental motion, it may be entertained when any subsidiary motion is pending, assuming that the situation calls for such emergency action.

Thus, whenever a member moves to lay a matter on the table, the Chair must immediately do two things:

a. Determine the intent of the member. The situation in which the motion is offered will usually make this intent clear with no problem.

b. Make the nature of the motion clear to all of the members. The Chair could say,

"It has been moved and seconded to lay this matter on the table. Since the intent of this motion seems to be to kill or dispose of the main motion, discussion is in order, and that discussion may go into the merits of the main motion. Is there any discussion?"

Or, in the other situation, the Chair could say,

"It has been moved and seconded to lay this matter on the table. Since the intent of this motion seems to be to defer action out of courtesy to our speaker, and since we can later vote to take the matter from the table, we will take an immediate vote."

Notice that many authorities, including *RONR*, classify this emergency motion to lay on the table as the most powerful of the subsidiary motions. You will find the complete discussion of the motion under that heading in these handbooks. Your understanding will be better, however, if you think of it under the heading of incidental motions.

2. *The Motion to Divide a Question*

Occasionally a motion may consist of several independent proposals, each of which would be viewed differently by the group. Perhaps a committee recommends two or three different courses of action, and the Chair of the committee combines all of these into one motion to approve all the resolutions. In this event, a member could rise, gain the floor, and say,

"I move that we consider each of those recommendations separately."

This motion requires a second, is voted on immediately without discussion, and is passed by a simple majority vote. The motion must always specify the precise way in which the basic question is to be divided. It may only separate truly independent parts of the original motion. In other words, the acceptance or rejection of any one part would have no effect upon the part or parts remaining. If this motion is passed, the Chair then permits discussion and a vote on each part of the original motion, as specified.

This motion need not be used when the original main motion to be divided consists of two or more completely independent resolutions, each dealing with a different subject. Such a motion must be divided at the request of any single member. This demand could be made by an individual even when someone else has the floor. The individual would rise and say,

"Madam Chair, I call for a separate vote on the first resolution."

The Chair should honor this request, permitting discussion and a vote on the first resolution separately from all the others.

3. *The Motion to Consider a Document by Paragraph or by Section*

At times, the main motion calls for the adoption of an entire document, perhaps a new set of bylaws or a policy statement of some sort. In this case, a member could gain the floor and say,

"I move that we consider these items by paragraph."

Or, more technically, she might say,

"I move that we consider these items seriatim" (pronounced "see-ri-**ate**-im").

This motion requires a second, cannot be debated, and passes by a majority vote. If the majority agrees to the procedure, someone (usually the Chair) reads each section in turn, opens it to discussion and amendment, and then moves to the next section. Finally, the entire document would be open to discussion and amendment. At the end, one vote would be taken to adopt or to reject the document.

This procedure of considering long documents section by section is so efficient that the Chair may propose it himself upon his own initiative. If no one objects, he would then proceed to discussion and amendment, section by section, with one final vote at the end.

4. *The Motion to Suspend the Rules*

Sometimes the strict obedience to the rules of parliamentary procedure or the customs of an organization may slow a meeting or cause confusion. Then a motion to suspend a particular rule would be helpful. A member could gain the floor and say,

"I move that we suspend the rules in order to proceed with item 14 in our agenda, out of its proper order."

This motion requires a second, cannot be debated, and ordinarily requires a two-thirds vote. Once it is passed, the Chair would proceed to whatever action the motion demanded.

Keep in mind, however, that certain "rules" can never be suspended. The constitution or bylaws of an organization, for example, are always in effect. They may be amended, but they cannot be suspended. Again, any rule serving to protect absentees could not be suspended.

On the other hand, some rules deal with administrative procedures rather than with parliamentary law. Such a rule, for example, might set the time at which a meeting ordinarily begins. A rule of this type could be suspended by a simple majority vote.

5. *An Appeal of a Decision by the Chair*

The presiding officer of any group does not enjoy unlimited power to make parliamentary decisions. The statement of a fact or a truth cannot be appealed, although its accuracy might be questioned. But rulings that pertain to such matters as the germaneness of an amendment would be subject to this motion. A member who questions the ruling would rise and, even without waiting to be recognized, would say,

"I appeal from the decision of the Chair."

This motion must be made immediately upon the announcement of the decision. It requires a second, since one member does not have the power to force a vote on the matter. Once a second is offered, however, the Chair is forced to submit her decision to the vote of the group.

This motion is usually debatable, the only incidental motion that permits discussion. The Chair has the privilege of speaking first, to defend her position, and she need not leave the Chair to do so.

According to *RONR*, other members are permitted to speak only once on this motion, either supporting or opposing the Chair's decision. Finally, the Chair is permitted to speak a second time, last of all, to respond to the opposition. These rules about speaking, however, assume that the Chair's decision and the resulting appeal take place when some debatable motion is before the group. If the decision and the resulting appeal happen to be made at a time when discussion is not in order, for example when the members have already voted to put an end to discussion of the motion at hand, then only the Chair could speak once, giving reasons for her decision. Then the matter must be put to a vote:

"Those who wish to sustain the decision of the Chair indicate by saying 'aye.' Those who wish to overrule the decision of the Chair indicate by saying 'no.' "

In case of a tie vote, the ruling of the Chair is sustained, since only a majority vote could overturn such a decision. Once again, the Chair could cast a vote to create a tie.

6. *The Motion to Create a Blank in a Pending Motion*

Occasionally a motion or an amendment may contain names, dates, places, or numbers that become the center of controversy. For example, suppose that the motion involves the donation of a sum of money to a specific mission. Some feel the amount is too great; others, that it is too small. A series of amendments trying to change the amount would involve the group in endless parliamentary red tape, with motions and seconds and votes, one after another. A simpler way to handle the situation is simply to create a blank in place of that sum of money and then to proceed to fill the blank. A member could gain the floor and say,

"I move to create a blank in the motion by striking out the sum specified."

This motion must be seconded, but it cannot be discussed. A majority vote is required to pass it. The whole procedure is so useful that the Chair may, on his own authority, suggest the creation of the blank and put the matter to an immediate vote, usually asking general consent.

Once a blank has been created, the next problem is to fill it. The procedure is essentially the same as in receiving nominations to fill an office:

a. The Chair calls for items to fill the blank.

b. The items suggested or nominated are listed.

c. The items are placed in order. In the case of names, the order is simply the order in which the nominations were made. In the case of numbers, dates, or places, the principle to follow is to place the one least likely to be acceptable first. In our case of donating money, the largest sum would be the one least likely to be acceptable.

d. The Chair calls for an "aye" and a "no" vote on each item in turn, following this order:

"All those in favor of the sum of $500 indicate by saying

'aye.' Those opposed say 'no.' The 'no's' have it, and that sum will be eliminated."

The Chair would then proceed to the next sum in the order, taking a vote in the same manner, until one item finally receives a majority vote.

e. The first item to receive a majority vote fills the blank. All of the other items, names, numbers, dates, and so on, are then automatically dropped with no further action. The blank in the main motion having been created and filled by this procedure, that motion would be open to further discussion and amendment.

7. A Request to Withdraw a Motion

When a motion is first made, it naturally belongs to the member who made it. In that brief interval when the motion is being heard and seconded, it belongs to the maker. She may withdraw it or modify it as she sees fit. However, once the motion has been stated by the Chair, it belongs to the entire membership, and no change may be made without majority permission. The maker of the motion must then rise, address the Chair, and say,

"Mr. President, I ask permission to withdraw my motion."

This request would be in order, even when another member has the floor. Technically, it is an incidental motion requiring a second and a majority vote. However, the efficient way to handle it would be for the Chair to ask for general consent:

"If there is no objection, Mrs. Smith will be permitted to withdraw her motion. (Pause) There is no objection; the motion is withdrawn."

If someone objects, the Chair should put the motion to an "aye" or "no" vote.

8. *Motions Incidental to Voting*

Any action in regard to voting would fit under this classification. The group may wish to determine the method of voting, perhaps by secret ballot or by roll call. Members may wish to close the polls or to reopen them. When an election is pending, the group may wish to determine the method of making nominations, to declare the nominations closed, or to reopen the floor for further nominations. All of the actions require an individual member to gain the floor, state the motion, and get a second. None of these motions would be debatable. Most of them would be passed by majority vote. However, the motions restricting the rights of the members, particularly the motion to close the polls or the motion to close nominations, would require a two-thirds vote to pass.

9. *Requests, Inquiries, and Demands*

A whole group of actions can be classed as incidental motions, although they are not really motions, in that they rarely require a vote or any action on the part of the group. They are, however, very useful mechanisms, and the Chair (as well as the members) should be familiar with all of them. These include:

a. The point of information. A member rises, perhaps even when someone else has the floor, and asks for information:

"Mr. Chair, I rise to a point of information."

The Chair then asks the member to state his point and tries to see that the needed information is provided.

Or the member may say,

"Mr. Chair, I would like to ask the speaker a question."

If the member speaking consents to this interruption, the question would then be asked and answered. If the speaker does not consent, the question would wait until the speaker is finished.

The point of information can be a useful device for correcting the Chair or another individual making a mistake in procedure while avoiding a direct confrontation. Having risen to a point of information, one might ask,

"Is the Chair aware that this present motion is not debatable?"

Raising a gentle question in this manner could call the attention of the Chair to his mistake and enable him to correct it.

b. A point of order. When it becomes absolutely necessary to point out a mistake in parliamentary procedure or in the rules of the assembly, a member could rise and say,

"Madam Chair, I rise to a point of order."

The Chair would then ask the member to state the point, after which the Chair would rule it "well taken" or "not well taken," giving her reasons. The Chair's ruling on the point would then be subject to an appeal, the fifth of the incidental motions discussed previously.

c. A parliamentary inquiry. This is another form of the point of information, with the information desired being of a parliamentary nature. The member may be asking, "Would an amendment be in order at this point?" The Chair would ordinarily supply the information desired. However, since the Chair is giving an opinion and not a ruling, no appeal would be possible.

The parliamentary inquiry often takes the form of the question, "Exactly what motion is before us at this time?" Members frequently raise this question just before a vote is taken. Like any other parliamentary inquiry, this query deserves a clear and immediate response. It should also serve as a warning to the Chair. If he is doing his job carefully, the members should not be confused about the motion at hand.

d. A division of the assembly. This request would come immediately after any vote by voice or by show of hands. Any member may make the demand by calling,

"Division!" or *"I call for a division."*

This demand forces the Chair to repeat the vote, this time by asking those in favor and those opposed to indicate their votes by rising. Technically, the Chair need not count the vote in response to this demand. However, while those voting in the affirmative are still standing, the Chair should count them. When the negative voters are asked to stand, the outcome of the vote may be obvious. If not, the Chair already has the affirmative count and can proceed to count the negative and announce the results with no further problems.

Any individual member has the right to use this demand to force the Chair to change from a voice vote to a rising vote. However, individual members cannot force the group to take ballot votes or roll call votes. A member might move that a given vote be taken by ballot, but this motion, another incidental motion, would require a second and a majority vote, with no discussion permitted. The Chair has the power of deciding to count a rising vote upon his own initiative, but he can only be forced to do so by a motion and a majority vote. The Chair would not have the power, on his own, to insist upon a ballot vote or a roll call vote. However, if the bylaws provide that a specific vote, perhaps to elect officers, must be by ballot, the bylaws must be obeyed. Not even a unanimous vote can override the requirements of the bylaws.

e. To raise a question of privilege. A member would use this mechanism to call the Chair's attention to a problem of heating, ventilation, noise, lighting, or other problem affecting the comfort of the assembly and the ability of the members to function in the meeting. Under such conditions, the member would rise and say,

"Madam President, I rise to a question of privilege affecting the assembly."

The Chair would then inquire about the problem and take whatever action is necessary to correct it. If some members object to the proposed action, the member affected would be permitted to introduce a motion that the action he desires be taken. This motion would be considered immediately, but it would be treated like a main motion, requiring a second, being open for discussion, and passing by a majority vote.

The complete discussion of this rather complex motion or request will be found in *RONR*, but it is listed there under the heading of "Privileged Motions." However, the Chair who thinks of it as simply another request, one incidental to the discomfort or lack of well being of the membership, should be able to handle it without difficulty.

Think of these requests, inquiries, or demands as occasions for the members to help you, the Chair, with your duties of presiding over the meeting. They all represent things you need to know—that someone is confused and needs information, that you may be making a mistake in proper procedure, that a member needs advice about the parliamentary situation, that there is a question about the outcome of a vote, or that someone is disturbed by noise or not hearing clearly. These are all opportunities for you to be of service to your members and to be more effective in presiding over the meeting.

HANDLING PRIVILEGED MOTIONS

Privileged motions do not relate to pending business but represent group actions so important that they may interrupt anything else, even incidental motions. *RONR* lists five of these motions (pp. 217-46). We have already included one, the "question of privilege" as an incidental motion. Another, which is intended to enforce the agenda in a meeting, is rarely necessary. Its objective can be achieved by a simple "point of order." This leaves us with three privileged motions, which, in theory, might sometimes be helpful.

1. *The Motion to Recess*

A member would rise, in the middle of the discussion of some matter, be recognized, and say, *"I move that we recess for five minutes,"* or *"I move that we recess until 8:15."*

These motions assume that the recess will take place immediately and that some other motion is pending at the time they are made. Under these conditions, they are privileged motions, require a second, and are put to an immediate vote, without discussion. A majority vote would pass them, and the Chair would then declare the recess as indicated.

A motion to recess made when no other matter is pending, or a motion to take a recess at some future time, would not be a privileged motion at all, but would be treated like any other main motion.

2. *The Motion to Adjourn*

A member who desires to terminate the meeting would rise, be recognized, and say,

"I move that we adjourn."

This motion requires a second and an immediate vote, without discussion. If it passes by majority vote, the Chair would be required to declare the meeting adjourned, even though all business has not yet been completed. Unfinished business would then go on the agenda for the next meeting. Before declaring the meeting adjourned, however, the Chair could make any necessary announcements.

This privileged motion to adjourn has some of the flavor of emergency action. The set time for adjournment has arrived or the business of the meeting has come to an end. Therefore, this motion cannot be qualified in any way. A motion to adjourn in ten minutes or a motion to adjourn at 9:00 P.M. would lose all privilege and be a main motion, with the low precedence of main motions, and open to discussion. Or if this happens to be a mass meeting, the assembly of a group that has no provision for a future meeting, the motion to adjourn also would become a main motion.

This motion is often unnecessary. If a scheduled hour to adjourn has arrived, or if all of the scheduled business has been completed, the Chair has the power simply to declare the meeting adjourned, without a motion coming from a member.

3. *The Motion to Fix the Time to Which to Adjourn*

If the motion adjourning the meeting comes before all business has been finished, and if some of these items must be settled before the next scheduled meeting of the organization, the members may wish to create an adjourned meeting. Such a situation would arise after a motion to adjourn has been passed. Therefore, this motion to set the time and perhaps place of an additional meeting is granted high privilege, so that it may be made at the last minute, just before the Chair actually declares the meeting adjourned.

Recognizing the need for such an emergency meeting, a member would rise, gain the floor, and say,

"I move that when we adjourn, we adjourn to meet here, this coming Friday night at 7:30."

This motion would require a second, could not be discussed (although it might be amended in regard to time or place), and would pass with a majority vote. In the situation we are describing, the Chair would announce the result of this vote and then declare the present meeting adjourned.

When the group gathers again for this adjourned meeting, at the specified time and place, the new meeting is technically a continuation of the previous one. Following the call to order, the secretary would be asked to read the minutes of the previous meeting, so that the record can be checked and so that everyone will remember the previous business. Then the group continues, just as though no time had elapsed.

Remember that this powerful motion is only for emergency use. The meeting is coming to an end, and the business at hand cannot be completed in the time remaining. Still, the matters being discussed are important items that cannot be put off until the next meeting. Under these conditions, the group needs to be able to set a new time and place to continue the present meeting. This motion to fix a time and perhaps a place to continue the business at hand could be essential under the circumstances.

However, if there is no emergency—that is, if this motion to create an adjourned meeting is made when no other business is before the meeting or in an assembly that already has plans for another meeting later the same day or the next day, this motion loses its privilege and becomes a simple main motion. The group always has the power to schedule an additional meeting for itself, but the normal way of doing so would be through the adoption of a main motion.

These three privileged motions are similar to subsidiary motions, in that they have a rank or precedence among themselves. The motion to recess is the weakest. It could be replaced by a motion to adjourn. However, the motion to recess would be out of order when the motion to adjourn is pending. The privileged motion to fix a time to which to adjourn is the most powerful of the three, as we have indicated.

As a general rule, all subsidiary motions take precedence over main motions, since their purpose is to refine the main motion. Within the group of subsidiary motions, each has its own power or precedence.

Privileged motions enjoy special power or privilege because of their emergency nature and would be in order at almost any time in the meeting. Each of these has its own power or precedence in respect to the others.

Incidental motions arise out of specific situations, and each has the power to be utilized whenever the situation demands, even if a privileged motion happened to be pending at the time.

As an extreme example, imagine that you are presiding in a situation in which a main motion is being discussed. Someone proposes an amendment. You accept this motion, get a second for it, and open it for discussion. While this change in wording is being debated, a member moves to send the whole matter to a committee for further examination. Again, you would get a second for this motion and open it for discussion. While the group is discussing this, another member moves to postpone the whole thing until the next meeting. You would accept this motion also as being in order. Yet another member, knowing that the hour is late, the discussion has gone on too long, and plans for the evening's program are being disrupted, moves that the whole thing be laid on the table. You would recognize that this motion is intended to meet the emergency in the time schedule, so you would accept it, get a second, and restate this motion to table, intending to put it to an immediate vote.

Before you can take the vote on this motion, however, someone else moves to adjourn. This motion would also be in order, so you would get a second and restate it, preparatory to voting. But even now, before you can take this vote, a member rises, gets your recognition, and moves to create a new meeting ("that when we adjourn, we adjourn until next week at this same time"). Assuming that each of these motions is seconded, all of this action would be quite proper and according to good parliamentary procedure. As the Chair (probably depending on the secretary to jog your memory), you would then proceed in reverse order, taking a vote on each action in turn until one of the votes brought an end to the series.

To carry this parliamentary nightmare a step further, imagine that you take a vote on the last of these motions made, the one to create the adjourned meeting. The resulting vote is very close, but you feel reasonably certain that the motion has passed. When you state this conclusion, even then a member could call, "Division!" This incidental demand would be in order and would force you to repeat the last vote, asking members for and against to rise.

All of these procedures are quite reasonable and not nearly as complex as they might seem from this description. If you remain cool under fire, you should have little difficulty, even in the most complex parliamentary situations. Probably the only thing you need, besides good common sense, is the order of precedence of the subsidiary motions. A simple chart, like the one included in this text, will solve that problem for you.

SOME SPECIAL MAIN MOTIONS

The motions we include here represent varieties of main motions, and the rules for considering main motions generally apply to all of them. However, each has some special features requiring particular knowledge and attention on the part of the Chair. You will find a detailed discussion in *RONR*, "Motions That Bring a Question Again Before the Assembly," pp. 294-329.

1. *The Motion to Take a Matter from the Table, or to Resume Consideration*

You will remember that under emergency conditions a member may move to lay a matter on the table. If this motion is seconded and passed by majority vote (with no discussion permitted), it clears away all pending motions in order to handle the emergency. Once that emergency is past, however, the assembly needs some mechanism to use in bringing those previously pending motions back to the floor once again. The motion to take a matter from the table supplies this mechanism.

The member wishing to bring that earlier motion or motions before the group again would rise, gain the floor, and say,

"I move that we take from the table the matter of . . . ." or *"I move that we resume consideration of . . . ."*

This motion would require a second and a majority vote. However, in contrast to other main motions, it is not debatable. Remember that the purpose of placing a matter "on the table" and taking it "from the table" again is to put that action aside to meet some emergency. Under such conditions, the group must act as efficiently as possible to set the matter aside and to take it up again. Thus no discussion is permitted in regard to either action. Obviously, this motion to take from the table could not be amended, since only the two alternatives (accept or reject) are possible. If this motion passes, the item to which it refers would come before the group again in precisely the same form that it had before it was placed on the table or postponed.

This motion would ordinarily be offered immediately following the emergency that caused the original motion to be laid on the table in the first place. However, it might be offered later in the meeting or even in the next regular meeting, assuming that the group meets as often as quarterly. Beyond the next session, the matter laid on the table is forgotten, and it could only be brought before the group again as a new main motion.

2. *The Motion to Reconsider Action Previously Taken*

If your group follows *RONR* as its parliamentary authority, this motion is theoretically possible.

However, its various rules and requirements are so complex that you would do well to avoid it. (In *RONR*, the discussion continues for twenty pages, pp. 309-29.) For example, note the following requirements:

a. The group cannot reconsider actions that are already being carried out. Once the group enters a contract, for instance, it could not reconsider that contract.

b. The one making the motion to reconsider must have voted on the prevailing side on the original motion. Other authorities disagree on this requirement, since it forces a member to reveal how she voted on the original motion.

c. The motion to reconsider can only be offered on the same day or the next calendar day as the original motion to be reconsidered.

d. The motion to reconsider has a double precedence, one power for the making and seconding of the motion and another for the consideration of the motion. Essentially, the motion could be made at any time in the meeting, and the Chair would then ask for a second. But the consideration of the motion has the precedence of the original motion to be reconsidered.

e. The motion is debatable, and it also opens the original motion to further discussion.

f. If the motion to reconsider is passed by majority vote, it returns the original motion for the consideration of the group, just as though the original vote had never been taken.

In view of all of these complications and because

authorities disagree on some of the details, you should suggest the use of the motion to rescind in place of the motion to reconsider.

3. The Motion to Rescind or Repeal Earlier Action

While we like to think that official action, once taken, will stand for all time, groups sometimes change their collective minds or recognize that an earlier action was mistaken. Thus some motion is necessary to permit what has been done to be undone. The motion to rescind accomplishes this purpose without all the complications of the motion to reconsider.

Any member should thus have the power to rise, gain the floor, and say,

"I move that we repeal the resolution passed at our last meeting in regard to . . . ."

This motion is a main motion and is only in order when nothing else is before the group. It requires a second, is debatable, and discussion may also go into the merits of the original question to which it applies. It may be amended; in fact, any of the subsidiary motions may be applied to it. Ordinarily, a two-thirds vote would pass the motion, following the principle that an action should stand unless a significant part of the group wants to change it. However, if advanced notice has been given prior to the meeting that the motion to repeal will be offered, a majority vote would be sufficient to pass it. Also, if the number of those voting to repeal an action happens to equal or be greater than the majority of the total membership of the group, that number would be sufficient to pass the motion, even without notice.

These rules would not necessarily apply to a repeal of any portion of the bylaws of the organization. Any change in the bylaws would require following the rules for amendment contained in the bylaws themselves.

COMMON
PARLIAMENTARY
PROBLEMS

By way of summary, here are some basic guide-lines that should be helpful to you in presiding over a group or in participating in a business meeting.

1. *Know the Precedence of Motions.*

Get rid of the old idea that "no two motions may be before the house at once." Any number of motions may be before the group at once, provided that each one offered has the power or precedence to replace the one already on the floor. If motion 1 is being discussed and a member makes motion 2, the Chair must know whether motion 2 has sufficient power to replace motion 1. If the power of motion 2 is high enough, the Chair will drop motion 1 and handle motion 2, only returning to motion 1 when the second motion has been completed. On the other hand, if motion 2 does not have sufficient power to displace motion 1, the member who offered motion 2 is declared out of order, and the group would return to the consideration of motion 1.

The following rules govern the precedence of motions:

a. One type of motion takes precedence over another. Thus subsidiary motions outrank main motions, privileged motions outrank all other types, and incidental motions have the power to replace whatever may be before the group when the occasion for them arises.

b. The assembly must consider main motions one at a time. Thus two main motions cannot be placed before the assembly at one time.

c. Subsidiary motions take precedence over one another in a very regular order:

> Amendments outrank motions to kill the main motion.
>
> To refer to committee outranks amending.
>
> Postponing to a stated time outranks referring to a committee.
>
> Limiting discussion outranks postponing to a stated time.
>
> Ending discussion outranks limiting discussion.

d. Any incidental motion takes precedence over any other incidental motion. The last one made is the one considered first.

e. Privileged motions take precedence over each other in a very regular order, the motion to recess being the weakest. To adjourn outranks to recess, and to set a time for a new meeting outranks adjourning.

f. When one motion grows out of another (as when a motion to amend grows out of some subsidiary motion, or perhaps when an amendment is offered to a motion to set the time for a new meeting) it takes precedence over the motion out of which it grows.

Although these rules sound complicated, we can reduce them to a simple chart so that they may be seen at a glance.

TABLE OF PRECEDENCE OF MOTIONS
An easy guide to the important facts about common motions

TYPES OF MOTIONS		Types of motions are listed in order of precedence from highest to lowest. A second motion cannot be accepted unless it has a higher precedence than the motion already before the group.	REQUIRES A SECOND?	MAY BE DISCUSSED?	MAY BE AMENDED?	VOTE NEEDED
	PRIVILEGED	To fix the time of the next meeting (made when other business is before the meeting)	Yes	No	Yes	Maj.
		To adjourn (when it doesn't adjourn the assembly forever)	Yes	No	No	Maj.
		To recess	Yes	No	Yes	Maj.
	INCIDENTAL	Lay a matter on the table	Yes	No	No	Maj.
		Divide the question	Yes	No	Yes	Maj.
		Consider section by section	Yes	No	Yes	Maj.
		Suspend rules	Yes	No	No	2/3
		Appeal a decision by the Chair	Yes	Yes*	No	Maj.
		Create a blank	Yes	No	No	Maj.
		Withdraw a motion	Yes	No	No	Maj.
		Close nominations	Yes	No	Yes	2/3
		Reopen nominations	Yes	No	Yes	Maj.
		Requests, inquiries, demands	No	No	No	None

TYPES OF MOTIONS			REQUIRES A SECOND?	MAY BE DISCUSSED?	MAY BE AMENDED?	VOTE NEEDED
	SUBSIDIARY	End discussion ("previous question")	Yes	No	No	2/3
		Limit discussion	Yes	No	Yes	2/3
		Postpone to a stated time	Yes	Yes	Yes	Maj.
		Refer to a committee	Yes	Yes	Yes	Maj.
		To amend an amendment	Yes	Yes	No	Maj.
		To amend a motion	Yes	Yes	Yes	Maj.
		Postpone indefinitely ("to kill")	Yes	Yes**	No	Maj.
	MAIN	An ordinary main motion	Yes	Yes	Yes	Maj.
		To take a matter off the table	Yes	No	No	Maj.
		To reconsider action previously taken	Yes	Yes**	No	Maj.
		To repeal action previously taken (to rescind)	Yes	Yes**	Yes	***

*May be discussed, but each member may speak only once.

**Opens the main question to discussion as well.

***Majority vote if proper notice has been given. Otherwise, 2/3.

2. Understand the Significance of the "Second."

The purpose of the "second" is to save the assembly from spending time on some proposal that only one person favors. The fact that someone else will second a motion indicates that at least two people favor its discussion. If most of the members of a group are obviously in favor of the motion, the Chair can save time by omitting the call for a "second." A resolution recommended by a committee, for example, would have the majority of the committee behind it. Normally this would mean at least two members support it, so the Chair should open that resolution for discussion without waiting for a second to be expressed.

Certain actions, however, are of such nature that only one person needs to favor them in order to force the Chair and the assembly to consider them. If the sound system has malfunctioned so that one person cannot hear, that individual should rise to a question of privilege, even without a second, and the Chair should take steps to remedy the situation. These actions, which do not require "seconds," are the ones we have listed as "Requests, inquiries, and demands."

Do not assume that the one who "seconds" a motion necessarily favors it. The act of seconding merely indicates enough interest that the proposal should receive the group's attention. The one who seconded a motion may actually speak against it and vote against it. In fact, after a motion has been revised through the amendment process, the one who originally offered the motion may finally vote against it.

While motions may require seconds, nominations do not. Don't confuse ordinary business meetings with political conventions. When candidates are nominated in a convention, seconding speeches are in order, largely to provide speaking opportunities for supporters of each candidate. Business meetings of ordinary societies are different. No seconds are necessary for candidates being nominated for office or for suggestions being offered for filling blanks in a motion.

3. *Promote Free and Open Discussion.*

As a general rule, all actions proposed for the group should be open to thorough discussion and debate before being decided by a vote. The Chair would usually first recognize the one making the motion. Then the floor should alternate between those favoring and those opposing the motion. No one should speak a second time until all who wish have spoken the first time. The old rule was to limit each member to two speeches on a given motion, with no speech longer than ten minutes. However, modern meetings rarely involve such long speeches. The Chair should permit brief comments on the motion and allow the members to say what they have to say, rather than limit discussion arbitrarily.

In a formal business meeting, the Chair does not participate in the discussion. If you are presiding and want to participate in this exchange, you must ask someone else, perhaps the vice-president, to preside so that you may speak. You must not, then, resume the Chair until the matter has finally been decided by a vote.

For the sake of efficiency, a few motions are not debatable. These include all of the privileged motions that we have listed, all of the incidental motions except the appeal from a decision by the Chair, and the subsidiary motions to limit or to end discussion. While the motion to appeal from a decision of the Chair is debatable, only limited discussion is allowed. Each member may speak once, but only once, to this motion. However, in this case the Chair may participate, speaking first and last in defense of the ruling that is being appealed. This is the only situation in a formal meeting when the Chair may argue the case without asking anyone else to preside.

This ban on discussion of certain motions does not stop the Chair or any member from making explanations or giving information that the group needs in order to vote intelligently on the question. Neither does this ban prevent a member from offering a motion of higher precedence than the one before the group. For example, you may be presiding when a member moves to create an adjourned meeting the next day. This motion is seconded. Then another member rises and addresses the Chair. You remember that the motion to fix the time of the next meeting, which has just been made, is the most powerful of the privileged motions and is not debatable. Thus you are tempted to refuse the floor to this member, to ask her to sit down, and to proceed to an immediate vote on the motion. But to yield to this temptation could be a serious mistake. The motion to fix the time of the next meeting is amendable, and that member may be rising to amend the motion to read "next Tuesday" instead of "tomorrow." Such an amendment would be in order, would require a second, but would not itself be debatable. Your best course of action would be to ask this member why she wants the floor. She may have it in order to offer an amendment. She may not have the floor in order to argue for or against fixing the time proposed for the adjourned meeting.

Ordinarily, all discussion is confined to the one question being considered by the group. If an amendment is before the house, members may discuss the amendment but not the main motion to which it applies. The three exceptions to this rule are the motion to postpone indefinitely (that is, to kill the main motion), the motion to reconsider previous action, and the motion to rescind or repeal previous action. All three of these motions would also open the main question to which they apply for further discussion.

Be particularly careful of those seeking to impose improper limits on free discussion. Notice that our list of "requests, inquiries, and demands" does not include a demand for an immediate vote. The members who sit in their seats shouting "Question! Question!" when others are wanting to speak are out of order and lacking in courtesy. Your responsibility as Chair is to call them to order, insist that they remain silent, and let those speak who wish to do so. The one who wishes to bring an end to discussion must rise, address the Chair, be granted the floor, and then offer the proper motion to end discussion. This motion receives an immediate vote. If two-thirds of those present and voting favor it, discussion of the main question is brought to a halt.

4. *Understand Voting Procedure.*

First, be aware of voting as a privilege and which members may exercise that privilege. In a convention, only delegates properly certified by the credentials committee may vote. In an ordinary group, all members may vote. The fact that you were elected president of the group does not deprive you of the privilege. When the vote is by secret ballot, you may cast a ballot along with the others. When the voting is not secret, however, you should keep your opinions and your votes to yourself (thus preserving your friendships) unless your vote will make a difference. If ten members vote for a motion and five members against it, your vote will not matter. Voting "yes" would make no difference, since the motion passes anyway, and it could lose you five supporters. On the other hand, voting against the motion and with the five could be even worse, and equally futile.

But suppose that the vote is five favoring the motion and four against it. If you favor the motion, keep still. The motion passes anyway. But if you oppose the motion, you would have the right to vote against it. The count would then be five for and five against. With the group equally divided, the motion lacks a majority, and it fails. In similar fashion, if the original vote is five to five and you oppose the motion, you can refuse to vote, and the motion fails. But if you favor the motion, you could make the vote six to five, and the motion passes. If your vote will make a difference, you have the right to cast it. On the other hand, like any other member, you always have the right to refuse to vote.

The fact that you are presiding, however, does not give you a second vote. Suppose that you favor a motion that is going down to defeat, four to five. You might vote, making the count five to five. But in that case, you would not receive a second vote to break the tie. Thus the motion is going to fail anyway, and you should keep your feelings and your vote to yourself.

Only the votes that are cast are counted. One has a right to abstain from voting, but the abstentions do not ordinarily affect the outcome of the vote. Suppose that with ten people present in a meeting, a proposal receives only four affirmative votes. But when you ask for the "no" votes, only three people vote against the matter. In such a case, the motion passes by a vote of four to three, even though three people abstained. The secretary's minutes recording such a roll-call vote would indicate four people voting "yes," three people voting "no," and three people voting "present," so that the official record would indicate the presence of a quorum.

Majority vote means a majority of the votes cast—that is, one more than half, which is the case with almost all of the votes in ordinary meetings. But *majority* may have other meanings. The bylaws of an organization may call for a different majority under some circumstances. If a particular action requires "a majority vote of the members present," for example, or "a majority vote of the total membership," the count would be much different. In cases like this, an abstention would actually have the effect of a "no" vote.

Most motions may be passed by a simple majority of those voting. There are a few motions, however, for which a simple majority is not enough. These motions tend to remove some right of the minority. Therefore, they require a two-thirds vote to approve them. These motions include those which limit or end discussion (removing the minority right of free speech) and the motion to close nominations (removing the minority right to offer nominations).

The two-thirds requirement is not difficult to calculate. Remember to double the "no" vote. An "aye" vote, equal to or greater than the "no" vote doubled, will pass these motions.

5. *Know the Powers of the Chair*

While the Chair is elected by the members and is responsible to them, he also occupies a powerful position, the position of leadership. He is not a dictator, but he has the responsibility of seeing that the group proceeds fairly and efficiently in handling the business of the day. The effective Chair needs to know both the limitations and the potentials of his office.

Normally, the Chair does not participate in the discussion of motions. He does not vote, unless the voting is by ballot or in a case where he chooses to create or break a tie. He should never be a member of a nominating committee, although he might serve on other committees. His decisions are subject to appeal by the action of any two members, one moving the appeal and the other seconding it. If the Chair's decision is overruled by majority vote on an appeal, the Chair must abide by that decision of the membership.

These limitations, however, are greatly overshadowed by the powers the Chair enjoys. He calls the meeting to order and acts throughout to preserve an orderly meeting. He may call any member to order or even expel a disruptive member. While he does not ordinarily participate in discussion, he may defend any decision of his that is being appealed, speaking first and last, while ordinary members may speak only once on the appeal.

The Chair can assume certain customary motions

105

and put them to a vote, without waiting for a member actually to offer the motion. Such actions would include a vote on approving the secretary's minutes. The Chair can also put the motion to adopt a committee recommendation, to receive a minority report from a committee when someone objects to hearing it, to create a blank in a motion, to adopt an auditor's report, to permit a member to withdraw her motion, and to take any customary action if someone objects to doing it. In all of these cases, the Chair simply assumes a motion to do these things and puts this assumed motion to the vote of the assembly.

In certain areas, the Chair can act on his own authority, without any voting on the part of the members. If he is uncertain as to the outcome of a vote, he can order a counted vote without a motion to that effect. If candidates are being nominated for office and no one is offering further nominations, the Chair can simply declare the nominations closed. If nominations are being offered for membership on a committee and the number nominated does not exceed the openings on the committee, the Chair can simply declare these nominees elected, once the nominations are closed. If only one person is nominated for an office, and if the bylaws do not require a ballot vote, the Chair can declare that person elected, with no vote at all. Of course, if the bylaws require a ballot vote (and thus the possibility of a write-in vote), the Chair must uphold the bylaws and take the vote, even if only one is nominated.

The Chair has the power, on his own authority, to

consider a long resolution section by section, even without a motion or vote to this effect. The Chair can declare a meeting adjourned in an emergency or when the proper time for adjournment arrives, even without a motion to adjourn. In fact, the Chair can declare a recess without a motion, when the program calls for a recess and the time for that recess arrives.

In turn, members should show the proper respect for the Chair. They address the Chair and are recognized before speaking to the assembly. They direct all of their remarks to the Chair and not to one another. They recognize that the Chair has been elected to his position of leadership and that this election obligates all members, even those in the minority opposition, to give their elected leader their full cooperation for his term of office.

6. *Keep Your Members Informed.*

You will naturally want to see that all of your members are informed of the activities of the organization. They should receive adequate advance notice of all meetings, including the agenda to be followed. If possible, you may want to mail out copies of the minutes and of the treasurer's report following each meeting. Keep channels of communication open. But remember that the Chair has an even more serious obligation to keep the members informed at all times throughout the course of each meeting.

Each point of information or parliamentary inquiry

requires a clear and immediate response. As Chair, you may personally supply the information, or you may ask someone who has the needed information to provide it. Many times these inquiries can be anticipated by keeping members aware of the question being discussed, the matter about to be voted, what an "aye" or a "no" vote will indicate, and the result of any action taken by the group.

Once a motion has been presented and seconded, your first obligation is to state that motion for the assembly. This action has parliamentary implications, because at the point where the Chair states the motion, it becomes the property of the group and can only be changed with the permission of the majority.

This initial statement also serves an important informative function. Be certain that all of the members can hear and understand. Speak loudly, slowly, clearly, and with special attention to those in the back row. You also have an obligation to the member making the motion that you repeat it accurately. If there is a question about the precise wording of the motion, you may ask its maker to submit this motion in writing or to repeat it for the benefit of the secretary. Only when the motion is clear to all should you open the floor for discussion.

As you are now aware, the discussion of any main motion may involve a number of subsidiary motions. An opponent may wish to kill the main motion and may move to postpone it indefinitely. Others may offer amendments to change the wording. Some may wish to send the action for committee study or to postpone the vote until a later time. You will probably want a table of the precedence of motions handy, so that you know what is in order and what is not.

The wise Chair will also keep paper and pencil handy, noting down the subsidiary motions that are offered, in order to remember which is currently before the group for discussion and action, and which to take up next. As each vote is taken, give the standard announcement of the outcome: how the vote went, whether the motion is carried or lost, what will be done as a result of that vote, and the next item for the attention of the group.

Frequently, you may need to translate the proposals of your individual members into language that the whole group will understand. For example, the member who responds to the discussion of the main motion by moving "the previous question" is making the powerful subsidiary motion to end the discussion and proceed to an immediate vote. Your members are entitled to know that this is a motion to halt further discussion of the main motion and to cut off other subsidiary motions. It requires an immediate counted vote, and it must be supported by two-thirds of those voting in order to take effect. The old expression, "I move the previous question," or, "I call the question," is so widely misunderstood that a clear explanation from the Chair is essential. Some groups will even find these wordings so odd that no one will second the motion, even though several may favor it. Help the member by rewording the motion:

"The member is moving that we end discussion and put the question to an immediate vote. Is there a second to this motion?"

If a second is then offered, restate the motion as usual:

"It has been moved and seconded that we end discussion and put the question to an immediate vote. All of those in favor please rise." (Remember, this motion to end discussion requires a two-thirds vote to pass.)

The proposal of an amendment to a motion is often a source of confusion for the group. Remember that the amendment process represents an attempt to reword a motion in the best and most acceptable manner. When you ask the members to vote on an amendment, you are not asking them to adopt the motion itself but only to adopt another wording for the motion. Once the wording has been perfected, then the basic motion must be accepted or rejected. Be sure your members know that amendments to a motion only change wording, not policy.

The vote on an appeal of a decision by the Chair can also become very confusing. If you ask those who "favor the appeal" to say "aye," no one will know what to do. Instead, once the discussion of the point at issue has concluded and after you have made your final defense of your ruling, repeat the decision you originally made, and then say,

"Those who sustain the decision of the Chair indicate by saying 'aye.' " Then, *"Those who overrule the decision of the Chair indicate by saying 'no.' "*

Then announce the result of the vote in the usual

manner. Above all, always repeat a motion before taking a vote. Your members should know precisely the matter to be settled and the meaning of an "aye" or a "no" vote. If someone raises a point of information—"What are we voting on?"—it may be a most serious criticism of the manner in which you are conducting the meeting. Keep your members informed!

7. *Know the Role of the Parliamentarian.*

Most small groups function without the help of a parliamentarian. Following this book as your guide, you can probably preside very successfully without such help. However, you may discover that your organization has a member, perhaps a former Chair, who is familiar with parliamentary procedure and whom you would like to employ (with or without remuneration) to advise you on parliamentary problems. The fact that he holds membership in the organization should not change the way he is utilized—nor the fact that the laborer is worthy of his hire, unless he is willing to contribute his services. When one serves as parliamentarian, he does give up certain privileges of membership. The parliamentarian, like the Chair, should remain objective and should not participate in the general discussion of items coming before the meeting. If a vote is by ballot, the member-parliamentarian may cast his ballot along with the rest. But on other votes, he

111

should not vote at all, even in case of a tie. (The latest edition of *RONR* has more detailed information, pp. 456-58.)

Larger organizations may hire a professional parliamentarian to assist the Chair. If you are called upon to lead a group providing such assistance, make use of this expert at all stages of preparing and conducting the meeting.

Provide the parliamentarian with all of the needed background, copies of your bylaws, standing rules, and so on. Include him in your planning consultations. Try to predict and to discuss any possible problems you see emerging. During the meeting, keep the parliamentarian seated next to you, and be in touch through notes or whispered conversations in regard to the parliamentary problems arising. Perhaps the parliamentarian can prepare a chart showing the basic information on each motion—in order/out of order, second required, debatable/not debatable, amendable/not amendable, two-thirds vote needed. His pointing to the item should serve to remind you of the facts you need.

Primarily, the parliamentarian is your advisor. He never makes rulings but only gives you parliamentary advice so that you may rule. You should be the one to explain a parliamentary situation to the assembly; only on rare occasions should you call upon the parliamentarian to do this. Remember, however, that the parliamentarian is also an employee of the organization, since the group is paying for his advice. Therefore, make provisions for your members to confer with the parliamentarian at times, and expect him to object to anything you do that might infringe upon the rights of the group—although such objections should ordinarily be made to you in private.

8. *Be Certain You Have a Quorum Present.*

Organizations must defend themselves against unrepresentative actions by small groups that may dominate poorly attended meetings. Thus the bylaws of the society should specify the minimum number of members who must be present to transact business legally. Ordinarily, a quorum would be the majority of the membership, but the variations among groups are so great that each one should specify the quorum for itself.

Many church congregations adopt the policy of making the quorum the number of qualified members actually attending a properly called meeting. Note that the quorum refers to the number of members that must be present, not to the number voting on any one question, since any member has a basic right to abstain from voting on any question. A properly called meeting is one that has been announced sufficiently in advance to allow members to attend. Such an announcement should be a clear notification to all members, by whatever method is customarily used in your congregation.

In a committee meeting, the majority of the

committee members usually constitutes a quorum. One difficulty arises in counting ex-officio members of a committee. These members belong to the committee because of some office that they hold. For example, the president may be an ex-officio member of all committees except the nominating committee. Ex-officio membership means that the individual has all the rights and privileges of committee membership and is expected to offer motions, to participate in discussion, and to vote like any other committee member. However, in a case where the president is ex-officio a member of all committees but the nominating committee, he is probably not expected to attend all of these meetings. Still, he is a committee member as long as he holds the office of president, and he should be notified of all meetings, like any other member. Such an ex-officio member is not counted in calculating a quorum for the committee meeting.

Naturally, no meeting could conduct business without a quorum present. Once a quorum is present and the meeting begins, the quorum is assumed unless someone notices that members have left and the quorum is no longer there. If a member notices the absence of a quorum, she may rise to a point of order to that effect, although she should not interrupt a speaker in doing so. If the Chair notices the absence of a quorum, he should also point out the problem to the assembly. Discussion of an item could continue, but no official action on the item would be possible.

In the absence of a quorum, an organization may

only take four possible actions: Members may recess, adjourn, adopt a motion to fix the time to which to adjourn, or take steps to obtain a quorum. Any other action that the group takes without a quorum is taken at its own risk. It can only hope that the action will be ratified at the next meeting with a quorum present.

COMMITTEE MEETINGS

In large congregations most of the actual business of the church is conducted in committees. Indeed, some churches expect all proposals to go first to the appropriate committee before coming to an official board or to the total membership. The careful examination and discussion of each proposal in a smaller group should result in wiser action by the administrative body of the congregation.

Committees are of two types. Standing committees are those appointed for a period of time, usually annually, or for the same period of time the officers of the group hold office. The names and functions of these committees are usually given in detail in the bylaws or organizational guidebook. Special committees (sometimes called "ad hoc committees"), on the other hand, are appointed for a special purpose and cease to exist when that purpose is accomplished.

1. *Appointing Committees*

In theory, there are five methods by which committees can be appointed. These methods are discussed in detail in *RONR* (pp. 483-87).

a. Election by ballot. This is the method generally

used by church groups for appointing members to standing committees, a method sometimes required by the bylaws and which preserves the secrecy of the vote. Names are usually suggested by a nominating committee. Additional nominations may also be made from the floor. All of these nominees are then submitted to the membership for an election ballot. Those receiving a majority vote become members of the committees.

b. Nominations from the floor. The members nominate candidates for the committee in much the manner that we have described under "filling blanks." Once a list of nominees has been completed, the Chair takes an "aye" and a "no" vote on each candidate in turn, in the order in which these people were nominated. Those receiving a majority vote become members of the committee until all vacancies are filled. At that point the election is over, and the names of remaining nominees are simply dropped.

An obvious problem with this method is that those nominated last have a reduced chance of being elected. Another alternative would be to take a counted vote on all nominees, declaring those with the highest totals to be elected.

c. Nominations by the Chair. In this case the Chair announces her list of nominees for the vacancies on the committee, and the assembly approves the total list with one "aye" or "no" vote. A member who disapproves of a name on the list could move to strike out that name. If this motion carries by majority vote, the Chair would be forced to replace that nominee with someone else. But since this method gives the Chair the power of nomination, no member would have the right to add a name to the list or to substitute one name for another.

d. Appointment by the Chair. This is probably the most efficient method of staffing a committee. However, the Chair cannot assume this power automatically. It must be given to her, either by some statement in the bylaws or by the vote of the group in setting up the committee. It is customary for the committee member named first by the Chair in making these appointments to be the Chair of the committee.

In making these appointments, the Chair should bear in mind the function of the committee. If it is expected to take action, it should be as small as possible and consist only of those in favor of the action involved. If the committee is to discuss and deliberate, it should be large and all viewpoints on the subject concerned should be represented.

e. Appointment by the motion creating the committee. That is, the motion creating a special committee specifies that Mr. A, Mrs. C, and Miss D will constitute the committee. This motion could also specify the individual to chair the committee. While the motion is being discussed, any member could move an amendment substituting one name for another or could move to create a blank as to the committee membership.

2. *Preparing for a Committee Meeting*

The following suggestions should prove helpful to the committee Chair:

a. Get the necessary information from the secretary of the general organization. He should be able to furnish you with the following material:

The notice of the appointment of the committee.

The names of the committee members. Don't forget that you may also need addresses and telephone numbers.

The paper or matter referred to the committee.

The list of any instructions that the assembly is giving the committee.

The secretary or other officers of the general organization may also provide information or documents basic to the work of the committee.

b. Arrange for a meeting time and place as soon as possible. If you can, get the members of the committee together immediately after the meeting in which they were appointed to decide on the time and place for a committee meeting. Ordinarily, the majority of the committee members would constitute a quorum for the meeting, but try to find a time when all can attend.

c. Remind the committee members of this meeting by mail ahead of time, including an agenda for the meeting and copies of any documents the members need to study in advance. Follow up with a telephone reminder the day before the meeting. Remember that this meeting is unusual and therefore much more easily forgotten than the regular meetings of the organization. Be sure that ex-officio members are notified also.

d. Make a tentative plan for the discussion. The usual problem-solving procedure follows an outline like this:

A statement of the problem. Exactly what is the question that the committee is to discuss?

Definitions. How can the terms of this question be clarified for all of the committee members?

Analysis of the problem. What is the nature of the problem, and what are its causes?

Criteria for solution. What standards must any acceptable solution be expected to meet?

Tentative solutions that meet these standards. At this stage you may wish to encourage the members to use their imaginations for all kinds of suggestions, no matter how foolish some of them may appear to be.

A comparison and evaluation of these suggestions.

The selection of the best of these suggestions.

Narrow these suggestions to a final solution or program acceptable to the majority of the committee.

The suggestion and evaluation of specific methods for putting this solution or program into effect.

The formation of the specific recommendation to be taken back to the parent body.

The preparation of the committee report, ending with whatever resolutions the committee wants the group to adopt.

e. Prepare the meeting place to facilitate the work of the committee. The room should be well lighted and comfortable. If paper and pencils are needed, have them available. Tables may be helpful when documents and writing are necessary. However, the best arrangement to facilitate discussion is to put the group in a circle, not separated by any unnecessary tables or other barriers. The advantages of this pattern are that every group member is visible to every other group member, and no one feels left out.

f. Be a good host, even if the committee is not meeting in your home. Give some thought to refreshments, perhaps as the committee is gathering or perhaps later, as the meeting comes to a close. If the committee members do not know one another well, you may want to prepare name tags and to provide time for introductions and for people to get acquainted. Prepare to create an atmosphere that is businesslike, yet comfortable enough that even the most reticent committee member will feel eager to make a contribution.

3. *Leading the Committee Meeting*

a. Start the meeting as nearly on time as you can. If you begin late, you only prove to those who came on time that they came too early. At the next meeting they won't be on time.

b. Introduce the question or problem for the group. If you expect this committee to discuss a particular difficulty, state the problem to encourage the maximum of discussion. A question like "Should we have our annual pledge drive in February?" is almost impossible to discuss. We either should or shouldn't. Both sides of the question might be presented, a vote taken, and the whole matter settled with no opportunity for a creative approach to fund raising. On the other hand, an open question such as "What form should our stewardship program take during the coming year?" would lend itself much more readily to creative discussion.

c. Clarify the question. Unless all of the members of the committee are acquainted with the background of the question, the reasons for discussing it at this time, the basic facts essential to its understanding, and the instructions given to the committee, they should be reminded of these things before the discussion starts.

d. Get the discussion underway. Up to this time, the Chair has been doing all of the talking. Now you want the committee to participate. Stimulate that participation. You might phrase a very specific question (probably concerned with the definition of the problem, following the outline that we have given) and ask the group in general for their answers. Or you might turn to one individual and ask for her ideas on the problem in general.

e. Be aware of committee variations in parliamentary procedure. You may wish to review the complete discussion in the sections of *RONR* which deal with the conduct of business in board and committee meetings (pp. 477-78 and 490-92). Members may speak while seated and may speak as often as they wish. Motions need not be seconded. Informal discussion is permitted while no motion is pending. The Chair may make motions and may participate in the discussion while continuing to preside. Motions to limit or to close debate are generally not permitted.

f. Don't dominate the discussion. The fact that you are the Chair and that you have introduced the committee to its work may tempt you to say too much. Never allow the feeling to arise within the committee that "This is the Chair's meeting; let him run it; let him talk, since he has decided everything anyway." Try to limit your contributions to those functions which only you as Chair can perform. These include:

Stating and introducing the question.

Supplying information not possessed by any other member of the committee.

Keeping the discussion centered on the subject at hand.

Raising questions to ensure that the entire subject is covered and that the discussion does not stagnate.

Encouraging the participation of all committee members.

Summarizing the discussion from time to time so that all members realize the aspects of the subject that are being covered.

g. Don't expect the committee to follow your

outline while discussing the problem. Members may add ideas or omit ideas entirely. The purpose of the outline is largely to help you keep discussion going and ensure that the subject is being covered. It should never be a straitjacket that binds the discussion. Don't expect every discussion to arrive at a solution to the problem discussed. Of course, if the discussion is in a committee meeting, and the committee must make a report, some sort of a conclusion will be necessary, even if it is only a listing of the information gathered. Sometimes the benefit of discussion comes from the exchange of views rather than the working out of solutions.

h. Encourage the reticent to participate. As a rule, the silence of the Chair is all the encouragement most committee members need. A few individuals may need to be called on by name for their views. The best method is to wait until the group is discussing some aspect of the problem that you know must interest this individual. Then call on him to give his reaction to some particular question. Ask a specific question, but be sure it is a question he can answer.

i. Keep the discussion on track. Don't let individual members of the group get off the subject unless the whole group, for some reason, wants to change the problem it is discussing. Note: Neither the statement of the problem nor the definition of terms needs to remain static throughout the entire period of discussion.

One of the best methods for keeping discussion on track is the internal summary. As Chair, find an appropriate spot to break off the discussion and summarize the progress the group has made to this point. The group should then see clearly the aspects of the subject that remain and should be eager to proceed to them.

j. Avoid arguments. Discussion is a process of pooling information, ideas, and viewpoints in order to solve problems and arrive at mutual understanding. Argumentation is the process of trying to bring another person to your particular viewpoint. No argument should be allowed until the group has decided on the two or three best solutions to the problem. Then the advocates of each solution may argue for it and leave the decision up to the vote of the committee.

One of the best methods for stopping an argument is also the internal summary. Again, you break off the argument and summarize the progress the group has made to this point. You indicate that the committee will simply have to "agree to disagree" on this issue and proceed to discuss other remaining areas.

k. End the discussion with a summary. Don't try to repeat every minor idea mentioned in the entire discussion. Rather, remind the group of the general areas of the subject covered and the consensus of opinion in those areas.

4. *Preparing the Committee Report*

When the committee finally decides on the particular action it wants taken, or information or advice that it wants to give to the assembly as a whole, it puts these conclusions in writing and adopts them by majority vote. This paper then becomes the report of the committee.

The report should generally follow this outline: First, give the name of the committee. Next, describe briefly how the committee went about its investigations. Third, summarize the facts or information the committee gathered. Some reports may end at this point, depending upon the purpose for which the committee was appointed. Usually, however, the committee report will go to the next step, giving the conclusions the committee has reached on the basis of the information gathered. Finally, the report will give the specific resolutions for the adoption of the assembly. This report should be in writing, clearly phrased in the third person (not "we did this" but rather "the committee did this"), and signed by the committee Chair. The words "respectfully submitted" are no longer considered in good form.

In giving this report, the committee Chair (or perhaps another reporting member) should read this document, which has been approved by the majority of the committee. If the report ended with resolutions, the reporting member should close by moving the adoption of these resolutions. Only one motion is necessary, covering all the resolutions, no matter how many. The assembly may divide this motion if it wishes to do so. The Chair of the assembly may also assume this motion to adopt the resolutions submitted by the committee. No second is necessary. The

Chair should immediately call for discussion and recognize the reporting member first to argue for the committee resolutions.

5. *Handling the Committee Report*

Once the committee report has been given, it is generally handled like any other main motion. Remember, however, that the proposed action is the adoption of the resolutions given by the committee. Avoid motions to "receive" the report or to "adopt" the report. "Receiving" a report makes no sense after the report has been given; in this case, the assembly has already received it. "Adopting" a total report would have the effect of endorsing everything the committee has reported, its procedure, the facts that it gathered, the conclusions it has derived. Such an endorsement is rarely necessary. If the committee is recommending certain specific actions, the motion before the assembly should deal with carrying out these recommendations. If the committee report is for information only and includes no resolutions, no further action is necessary.

One other common situation requires handling in a slightly different fashion. This is the case when a motion originated with the assembly and the subsidiary motion "refer to committee" was applied to it. When the committee finishes considering the matter and reports, the question for discussion is the original motion rather than the committee report.

Any committee considering a motion referred to it can come out with a limited number of possible reports. First, it may simply recommend the adoption of the motion. In this case, you would, as Chair, open the motion for further discussion, any subsidiary motions that members may wish to apply, and finally a vote. The recommendation of the committee would simply be considered as part of the discussion favoring the motion. Additional comments from individuals favoring or opposing the motion would be in order before the vote.

Second, the committee may recommend against the original motion. Nevertheless, as Chair you would open the floor for further discussion of the original motion and its adoption, "the recommendation of the committee to the contrary notwithstanding." Once again individual comments both pro and con would be welcome. You would finally take the vote on the adoption of the motion, in spite of the committee opposition.

Third, the committee may be unable to agree on any recommendation in regard to the original motion. If such is the case, you would again open the floor for further discussion of that motion. Your group would have no committee recommendation to consider, but the members would benefit from the committee's report of facts discovered and possibilities discussed in the committee deliberations. Presumably, the final vote of the group would thus be wiser.

Finally, the committee may recommend changes

or amendments in the original motion. The reporting member, ending his report, would then move the adoption of these amendments. (Only one motion covering a number of amendments would be required, but the assembly could then divide this motion if it wishes.) You would then open the floor for discussion and adoption of these amendments before accepting any new discussion or amendments. Once the committee amendments have been discussed and voted, one way or another, you would permit further discussion and possibly additional amendments of the main motion. The final vote on the main motion would come after the amendment process and any further discussion have been completed.

Occasionally, the minority of a committee will wish to submit a report that differs from the report of the majority. Remember that the minority report is nothing more than discussion of the recommendations of the majority; the committee report is always the report of the majority. Therefore, the minority report is not in order until the majority report has been read, a motion made for the adoption of its resolutions, discussion called for, and the reporting member recognized to defend the committee recommendations. At this point a representative of the minority might be recognized to present a minority report and perhaps move to amend the majority report by substitution of the minority report. If a member objects to hearing the minority report, a vote of the majority of the assembly to permit it is necessary before the minority report is read.

The most common difficulties in handling reports can be solved if you will remember some basic advice. Never permit a motion to "receive" a report after the report has been given. Take no action on reports given for information only. For example, a treasurer's report usually contains only information on the financial status of the organization. It requires no action but is submitted to the auditing committee at the end of the year. The report of a nominating committee is also informational. Take no action on this report, but proceed to the election process itself. If the report deals with a motion previously before the group, the question basically should be on the adoption of this motion. If the report brings new recommendations to the group, state the question on the adoption of these new resolutions.

ELECTING OFFICERS

One of the matters that should be clearly outlined in the individual bylaws of every organization is the procedure for electing officers. Of course, any procedure thus outlined should be followed by that group instead of the possibilities given here. These comments are only intended as guides for those points not included in the bylaws of your group.

1. *Nominations*

The first step in an election as carried out by most groups is the nomination of candidates for office. Strictly speaking, however, nominations are not necessary when the election is by ballot. Members may vote for any other member they please. The first individual getting a majority of the votes is elected. This method, however, may require a whole series of ballots before any individual receives a majority. As a rule, one of the six methods of nomination discussed in *RONR* (pp. 422-30) would be preferable.

a. Sometimes the Chair may make the nominations. This method may be followed in deciding on the personnel for a committee. It is not to be recommended for the officers of an ordinary society. As a general rule, the Chair should never be a member of a nominating committee, to avoid the danger of one clique controlling the organization, term after term.

b. Nominations from the floor would be a more usual procedure. Here, when the time for an election arrives, the Chair opens the floor for nominations. Any member may suggest a name, without waiting to be recognized. Seconds are not required.

The Chair should remember that the right to nominate for office is one of the fundamental rights of the minority. For that reason, the motion to close nominations requires a two-thirds vote. On the other hand, the motion to reopen nominations only requires a majority vote.

The motion to close nominations is never in order until sufficient time has been allowed for nominations from the floor to be made. But if sufficient opportunity has been given and no further nominations are being offered, the Chair may declare the nominations closed on his own authority.

c. Most organizations use the third method of nomination, the work of a nominating committee. This committee is appointed or elected to nominate a candidate for each office to be filled. The committee should never be appointed by the president, nor should the president be a member of it. The bylaws may require two or more nominees for each position, but one is usually advisable. The committee should question each individual to be nominated to be sure that he or she is willing to be a candidate before the nominations are announced in the committee report.

Occasionally, a committee will want to nominate one of the committee members for office. No rules prohibit the arrangement, although the committee member nominated may ask to be replaced on the committee before the nomination is announced. Once the committee reports its nominations, the Chair should ask for further nominations from the floor before declaring the nominations closed.

d. A fourth method involves the use of a nominating ballot. All members fill out ballots. Anyone mentioned on any ballot, without regard to the number of votes, is declared a nominee. This nominating ballot should never be declared the electing ballot, nor should the election be limited to the two nominees with the highest nominating totals. For this reason, the nominating ballot is a time-consuming procedure, since it must be followed by one or more additional ballots to decide the election.

e. The fifth method, nominations by mail, would rarely be used by church groups, since it assumes a widely scattered membership using the mails instead of meeting. It resembles the procedure used in the nominating ballot except that these ballots are submitted by mail.

f. The final method, which might be specified in the bylaws, is that of nomination by petition. In this case, a person could become a nominee for office upon presentation of a petition signed by a specified number of members. This method is sometimes used to supplement the work of a nominating committee.

2. *Elections*

There are several possible ways of voting on any question. One can use ballots, the simple voice vote of "aye" or "no," a roll-call vote, or some system of preferential voting.

a. Unless your bylaws state a different rule, the vote in an election should be taken by secret ballot. In this case, the members indicate their choice for the office by marking a ballot. These ballots are handed out and collected by "tellers" appointed by the Chair. The tellers also count the ballots, keeping track of the count on a tally sheet. The tellers must take every precaution to ensure the secrecy of the ballot and the accuracy of the count. After the election, ballots and tally sheet are turned over to the secretary for safekeeping until it is obvious that the election will not be contested.

In a ballot vote, a candidate must have a majority (more than half) of the total votes cast (not counting blanks) in order to be elected. Write-in votes should be counted. If no one has a majority, the vote for that office should be repeated. Nominees who receive low vote totals should not be dropped from the ballot unless they choose to withdraw from the contest. Remember that with a ballot vote the Chair casts a ballot along with the rest and does not receive a second vote in case of a tie.

b. In using a simple voice vote or a vote by show of hands, the Chair takes an "aye" and a "no" vote on each candidate in turn, in the order in which the candidates were nominated, just as in taking a vote on a motion. The Chair might say,

"All those in favor of electing John Jones to the office of secretary indicate by saying 'aye.' Those opposed say 'no.' The 'aye's' have it, and Mr. Jones is elected."

In this case, the first candidate to receive a majority vote is elected, and the other names are dropped. The obvious disadvantage of this method is that it fails to provide for secrecy in an election.

c. The roll-call vote follows the same procedure as voting by ballot, with the members casting their votes as their names are called and the secretary keeping track of the number of votes each nominee is receiving. Again, the voting would not be secret, but in a representative assembly the delegates may be obligated to inform their constituents of how they voted.

d. Preferential ballots are sometimes used to avoid the problem of repeated votes when no candidate receives a majority. They should only be used when the bylaws specifically provide for them. One method would be to ask all voters to fill out ballots listing the nominees in order of preference. The tellers then place these ballots in piles for each candidate, according to the first preference specified on the ballot. If no candidate has a majority at that point, the smallest pile of ballots is redistributed according to the second-choice candidate specified on each ballot. This process of eliminating and redistributing the smallest pile of ballots is continued until one pile of ballots has the majority of the votes cast. That candidate is declared to be elected.

3. *Motions Incidental to Voting*

The following motions have no particular bearing on the actual election, but they are frequently heard and should be properly handled by the informed Chair.

a. The motion to instruct the secretary to cast a unanimous ballot for a certain candidate or slate of candidates. This motion may only be admitted when the election is to be by a voice vote. It may only be passed by general consent—that is, the motion specifies a unanimous ballot, so one objection or negative vote is enough to defeat the motion. When the bylaws specify a ballot vote, this motion would not be in order.

b. The motion to make unanimous a vote that was not unanimous. This motion can be made only by the defeated candidate or his representative. It requires a unanimous vote. When the election was conducted by ballot, this motion also must be voted on by ballot.

c. The motion to close nominations and instruct the secretary to cast a unanimous ballot for the one candidate nominated. This motion should never be permitted. It confuses two different motions, one on the nominations and one on the election. It destroys the secrecy of the ballot, and it prevents members from offering write-in votes on their ballots.

USING PROPER FORMS

Many of the documents and records of any organization should follow a particular form or pattern. Although you cannot be expected to know these forms by memory, the information is occasionally very necessary. At such times the suggestions below should prove helpful.

1. *The Secretary's Minutes*

Write clearly, leaving a wide margin on the left to provide for additions or corrections. Begin with one paragraph, identifying the meeting and containing the following information:

   a. The kind of meeting (regular, annual, special, etc.).

   b. The name of the organization.

   c. The time, date (don't forget the year), and place of meeting.

   d. The fact that the regular Chair and secretary were present or the names of any substitutes.

   e. The reading and approval of the minutes of the previous meeting.

From this point on, each subject should be treated in a separate paragraph. The following items should be included:

a. A brief summary of the treasurer's report.

b. Mention of committee reports received. The complete written reports should be attached.

c. All main motions except those withdrawn. Note that defeated main motions are recorded.

d. All points of order and appeals, together with a summary of the reasons for each ruling by the Chair.

e. Secondary motions that were not lost or withdrawn. The secretary will need to keep careful notes of subsidiary motions, although these may receive only brief mention in the minutes. If a main motion happens to be postponed or if it is still undecided at the moment of adjournment, the secretary will need to make a complete report on pending subsidiary motions when consideration of that main motion continues.

f. It is not necessary to record the name of the one who seconds each motion. The name of the person making each motion should be recorded.

The final paragraph of the minutes should specify the time of adjournment. The signature of the secretary should be placed at the end of the minutes for each meeting. The words *respectfully submitted* are no longer considered in good form.

Additions and corrections are made in the wide left margin. When the minutes are read and approved, the secretary should write "approved" and the date on the left side of the page. This inscription should then be signed also.

The approval of the minutes is an important action

that should never be avoided, since it ensures the accuracy of the secretary's record. Some organizations save time by sending copies of the minutes to all members following each meeting. Then at the next meeting, the minutes can be corrected or approved "as distributed," without taking the time to read the entire document aloud.

When organizations meet infrequently, members have some difficulty in remembering the events of the previous meeting with sufficient accuracy to correct the secretary's record. The usual rule is to provide some other means of correction and approval, if there is a gap longer than three months between meetings. Some groups permit the executive committee to perform this function, and others appoint a special committee to approve the minutes. (*RONR* includes a detailed discussion of the minutes, pp. 458-66.)

2. *The Bylaws*

The basic document outlining the nature and form of an organization is now generally called the *bylaws.* The older term is the *constitution.* Some groups follow the custom of dividing some of this material into two documents, calling one the *constitution* and the other the *bylaws.* The only purpose served by this division would be to make the constitution more difficult to change than the bylaws, which seems unnecessary. In giving the form of the bylaws, we shall assume that it is a single document. You may wish to consult the chapter on bylaws found in *RONR*, pp. 559-92.

If an organization is to be incorporated, it will also have a corporate charter. This document should be drawn by an attorney to fit the legal requirements of the state. Naturally, the bylaws must be in harmony with that corporate charter.

The bylaws are usually organized as follows:

Article I. Name. This item may be omitted when the name is given in the corporate charter.

Article II. Object. The purpose of the organization should be specified in one sentence.

Article III. Members. Classes of membership, requirements of membership, etc., should be outlined here, probably in several sections.

Article IV. Officers. This section should name the office titles desired, their term of office, method of election, and the method of filling vacancies.

Article V. Meetings. Give the dates but not the times at which meetings are to be held. The article may also specify an "annual meeting" or a meeting at which officers are to be elected. Provision should be made for calling special meetings. The quorum for meetings should be specified.

Article VI. Executive Committee or Board of Directors. The composition and powers of this committee should be included. Other items might give rules under which the committee operates, its quorum, how often it meets, etc.

Article VII. Committees. The standing committees are listed here, giving the name, membership, manner of election, and duties of each. This article should also provide for the appointment of special committees as needed.

Article VIII. Parliamentary Authority. Since the bylaws and any special rules an organization may adopt are usually brief, the group should specify a more detailed authority as a guide in unusual situations (*RONR* is recommended). A published guide could be specified as the adopted authority for the organization. This article should also indicate that the parliamentary authority will only be followed when it is not inconsistent with the bylaws themselves.

Article IX. Amendment. This article gives the procedure for making changes in the bylaws. As a rule, amendments should require previous notice given in some specified manner, and an affirmative vote of at least two-thirds of those present and voting.

3. *Resolutions*

The formal resolution may begin with a preamble, which is a series of paragraphs giving the basis for the resolution. Each of these paragraphs should begin with the word *Whereas,* followed by a comma and the next word starting with a capital letter. Each of these paragraphs, except the last, should end with a semicolon. In the next to last paragraph, this final semicolon is followed by the word *and.* The final paragraph ends with a semicolon. This final semicolon is sometimes followed by the words *therefore, be it* with no punctuation at the end. However, these connecting words should be kept to a minimum. You will note that no periods are used in the preamble. A preamble should be used only to provide little-known information essential to the understanding of the resolution itself.

The resolution itself begins with the word *Resolved, That . . . .* The term *resolved* is capitalized, under-lined, and followed by a comma. *That* begins with a capital letter. If this is the first of a series of resolutions, it may end with a semicolon, followed by the word *and* without punctuation. Each of the following resolutions in the series would begin in the same manner. The final resolution in the series would end with a period.

A complete resolution might look something like this:

Whereas, The pastor returned early from his vacation last summer;

Whereas, The resignation of our youth minister has given the pastor some additional and time-consuming responsibilities; and

Whereas, These responsibilities and their related stress have placed the pastor's health in jeopardy;

<u>Resolved</u>, That the pastor's vacation period be extended by one week this year;

<u>Resolved</u>, That our pastor emeritus be paid to supply the pulpit on this additional Sunday; and

<u>Resolved</u>, That our youth committee be instructed

to begin interviews for a new youth minister at the earliest possible date.

When a committee wishes to recommend a particular action, that action is written as a resolution and placed at the end of the committee's report. The report then states that the committee recommends the approval of the following resolution, and the resolution is then read. The Chair would then open the floor for discussion of the resolution (committee proposals do not require a second) and normally assign the floor to the reporting member of the committee in support of the resolution.

GLOSSARY OF PARLIAMENTARY TERMS

Words and phrases in bold in the definitions are main entries.

Abstain—Not voting. Ordinarily, no one is forced to cast a vote, so abstention is a basic right. However, abstentions are not counted in determining the outcome of the vote.

Accepting—Accepting a report means the same as adopting a report. It means to give the report the approval of the group; to put it into action. Do not confuse these terms with **receiving** a report (merely listening to it). It is highly unusual to vote to receive or to accept a report. Once it has been heard, it has been received. Rarely does a group need to approve an entire report. Informational reports need no action at all. Any action taken should be upon the resolutions recommended in the report.

Ad hoc Committee—A special committee appointed to consider a motion or to carry out some special task. Once the work is done, this committee ceases to exist. It differs from a standing committee.

Adjourn—To bring a meeting to an end.

Adjourned Meeting—A meeting at a later time and place, which is legally a continuation of the previous meeting. (Compare **special meeting**.)

Adopting—To approve or accept, making something the rule or policy of the group. This is usually done by majority vote. Adopting a report means to give it approval or put it into action. (See **accepting**.)

Affirmative Vote—Voting "yes" or "aye."

Agenda—The official order of items to be followed in a meeting.

Amend—To change or modify. The motion designed to accomplish this change is called an amendment. To amend a motion is to change its wording and is not the same as adopting the motion.

Announcement of the result of a vote—The official announcement made by the Chair once a vote has been complete. It should include the outcome of the vote, whether the motion was adopted or lost, what will be done as a result of this vote, and the next item for the attention of the organization.

Annual Meeting—A regular meeting of the organization, at the beginning of its year, in which officers are elected and reports heard from officers and committees.

Appeal—A motion which questions a decision made by the **Chair**, asking that the assembly consider and possibly overrule that decision.

Approval of Minutes—The official act which certifies the **secretary**'s minutes as correct and makes them the official record of the meeting reported.

Articles of Incorporation—(See **corporate charter**.)

Assembly—The society, club, organization, etc.

Aye—(Pronounced "Eye.") Affirmative vote. "Yes."

Ballot Vote—A secret, written vote or expression of choice in most organizations. Secret votes by machine are also possible.

Board—A special kind of committee created in the **bylaws**. It usually is composed of certain members to govern an assembly or supervise its affairs between meetings of the general membership. It is sometimes called an executive board or board of directors.

Bylaws—Code of rules or regulations having more authority than ordinary rules of the organization. Ordinarily the term refers to the governing document of the society. Most groups now have one document which is called **bylaws** rather than **constitution.** Dividing this material into two separate documents is confusing and unnecessary.

Chair—The officer presiding over a meeting. The Chair should always refer to herself or himself in the third person, not as "I," but as "the Chair."

Commit—To turn a matter over into the care of a committee. (See **refer to committee**.)

Constitution—The governing document of the organization. Today usually called the **bylaws**.

Corporate Charter—A legal instrument describing the organization, which is filed with the appropriate state in the process of incorporation.

Debatable—Open for full discussion and argument.

Demand—An official request for action which one member can make on his own authority, without a second or a vote.

Division of a Question—An action which separates independent parts of a motion or resolution so that they may be discussed and voted on separately.

Division of the House—Sometimes called "division of the assembly." A demand made by any individual member to require a rising vote when the voice vote is not conclusive.

Ex-officio Member—A member of a committee or group by virtue of holding some special office. The Chair is often designated by the **bylaws** as an ex-officio member of all committees except the nominating committee. The ex-officio member has all of the privileges of membership but is not expected to attend all meetings.

Fix Time to which to Adjourn—A motion to set the time and place of an **adjourned meeting**, to continue the business of the present meeting.

Floor—The exclusive right to be heard at that time. A person has the floor when he has the right to speak. No one else may speak until he yields the floor or until the floor is given to another. A subject is on the floor when it is the substantive issue on which action is to be taken before any other matter may be discussed.

Friendly Amendment—An amendment to a motion that is thought to be acceptable to everyone, including the member who offered the original motion. This "friendly" change in a motion is usually accomplished with little discussion and approval by **general consent.**

148

General Consent—A voting procedure. An opportunity is offered for objections to a given motion or course of action. The fact that no objections are offered is considered as a unanimous vote in the affirmative.

House—The assembly or group.

Immediately pending—(See **pending.**)

Incidental Motion—a motion pertaining to incidental issues arising out of the pending question or the parliamentary situation, issues that must be settled in one way or another before further progress in the meeting.

In Order—Any action that would be permitted by the rules at that particular time in the meeting.

Lay on the Table—A motion to set a matter aside, under emergency conditions, to take care of some unforeseen circumstance that has arisen.

Limit Debate—A **subsidiary motion** that restricts the freedom of discussion on the motion or motions to which it applies. Limitations can be in the length of speeches, the number of speeches, or the total time allotted for discussion.

Main Motion—A motion that brings any particular subject before the group. The organization determines its policies and actions by adopting main motions.

Majority—More than half of the legal votes cast, ignoring blanks or abstentions.

Make a Motion—The formal act of offering a motion for the consideration of the group.

Meeting—The official assembly of the members of an organization to conduct business.

Minority—One half or less of the group. (Compare **majority.**)

Minority Report—The report of a **minority** of a committee, differing in some manner from the report of the majority—that is, from the official committee report.

Minutes—The **secretary's** record of the proceedings of a meeting.

Motion—A proposal by any one member for the consideration and action of the group. It should usually be introduced with the expression, "I move that . . . . "

Negative Vote—"No" vote.

New Business—Proposals for group consideration that have not been offered before.

Nominate—To propose for office. To list as a candidate for office. In ordinary groups, nominations are not seconded.

Notice—Also "give notice" or "previous notice." To inform the members ahead of time that a meeting will be held or that certain motions will be considered. The specific requirements for giving valid notice should be spelled out in the bylaws.

Objection—The formal expression of a negative view by any one member. Any such objection defeats a motion that must be unanimous and prevents any action by general consent.

Old Business—(See **unfinished business.**) This

expression **old business** should be avoided in favor of **unfinished business.**

Orders of the Day—Program or order of business.

Out of Order—Any proposal or action that would, at the moment, be contrary to the rules of the organization.

Parliamentarian—An expert in parliamentary procedure who serves as an advisor to the Chair on parliamentary matters.

Parliamentary Authority—The detailed manual of parliamentary procedure specified in the bylaws as the guide for the group in these matters.

Parliamentary Inquiry—To ask for information concerning some matter of parliamentary procedure.

Parliamentary Procedure—Sometimes called "parliamentary law." The rules or procedures governing deliberative assemblies.

Pending—Before the assembly for action, having been stated by the Chair and not yet disposed of in any way. When several motions are pending, the one last stated by the Chair is said to be immediately pending.

Plurality—A number of votes cast for a candidate in a contest of more than two candidates that is greater than the number cast for any other candidate, but not more than half the total votes cast.

Point of Information—An official request made to the Chair, for some bit of information vital to the continuation of the discussion at hand.

Point of Order—An official request to the Chair that the rules of order be followed. The point is raised when a member feels that some violation of the rules is taking place.

Postpone—A motion to defer action until a future time. The motion should always specify the time to which the item is deferred.

Postpone Indefinitely—The weakest of the subsidiary motions. Its effect is to kill the main motion to which it applies.

Precedence—(Pronounced "pre-**seed**-ence.") The order in which motions may be made and considered. A motion of high precedence may be made when a motion of lower precedence is pending, displacing the lower motion in receiving the attention of the group.

Present—Those physically in attendance at a meeting.

Present and Voting—Those present who actually cast a legal vote, in contrast to those abstaining from voting.

Previous Notice—(See **notice**.)

Previous Question—An old and confusing name for the motion to put an end to all discussion. This name frequently leads to misunderstandings and should be avoided. Rather, a member should move to stop discussion and vote immediately on the matter under consideration.

Privilege, Question of—A request that something be done to correct a situation that interferes with the rights or privileges of the assembly or of its individual members.

Privileged Motion—A type of motion that is not

related to the pending question but that is of sufficient importance to take precedence over all other types of motions.

Question of Privilege—(See **privilege, question of.**)

Quorum—The number of people or the percentage of the membership that must be present for the group legally to transact business.

Receiving—To permit a report to be heard by the group. Do not confuse this with **accepting** a report. Once a report has been given, it has already been received.

Recess—To take a short break in the proceedings, after which business resumes at the same point at which it was interrupted.

Recognition—The formal act by which the **Chair** grants the **floor** to a member wanting the attention of the assembly.

Reconsider—A complex motion used to nullify an earlier vote and bring the matter before the group once again.

Refer to Committee—A subsidiary motion that sends the pending question to a committee for more intensive discussion, investigation, or possibly for action.

Repeal—Also rescind. A motion used to nullify some earlier action.

Resolution—A formal motion, usually of some length, specifying the position or action of the organization. It begins with the words, *Resolved, That . . . .*

Rising Vote—A method of voting by which members

stand to express their preferences, first those in favor of the action, then those against. The **Chair** determines which side has the majority. If the vote is close, the **Chair** may count those standing for each vote.

Roll-call Vote—A voting procedure in which the **secretary** calls the roll and members respond by voting "aye," "no," or "abstain."

Rules of Order—The regulations adopted by the organization governing procedural matters in its meetings.

Second—An indication that another individual wishes an item to receive the attention of the group. It does not, however, necessarily indicate favorable support for that item.

Secretary—The officer who keeps the record of proceedings in a meeting. Along with the **Chair,** the secretary is one of the two essential officers for any business meeting.

Seriatim—(Pronounced "see-ri-**ate**-im.") Section by section or paragraph by paragraph. It is a method of considering a long document one section at a time, without actually dividing it into separate questions.

Show of Hands—A method of voting in which members indicate their preferences by raising their hands. In a large group, this method is no more accurate than a **voice vote.** However, in a small group, this method could substitute for a **rising vote.**

Special Committee—(See **ad hoc committee.**)

GLOSSARY

Special Meeting—An extra meeting of the organization, called according to the procedures for
creating such meetings, as specified in the **bylaws**.

Standing Committee—A permanent committee specified in the **bylaws** to carry out some regular
function of the organization.

Subsidiary Motion—A type of motion that is applied to
other motions (usually main motions) in order to
modify them to suit the wishes of the assembly.

Substitute—Replacing one part of a motion with
another, a type of amendment. The term *substitute*
is only used when the part in question is as long as
an entire paragraph or longer. For shorter sections
the better phrasing is *to strike out and insert*.

Suspend Rules—An incidental motion to permit some
specific action in violation of the usual rules of
order of the group. Note that the **bylaws** can never
be suspended in this manner.

Table—A common form of the motion to **postpone
indefinitely.** Its effect is to kill the main motion to
which it applies. Also a variation of the motion to
lay on the table. This is an emergency motion,
designed to set a matter aside to take care of
something more demanding.

Take from the Table—A motion to restore an item that
was placed on the table, once the emergency that
led to the tabling has passed.

Teller—A member appointed to assist the **Chair** in
conducting a vote, handing out ballots, collecting
them, counting them.

Tie Vote—Exactly the same number voting for and

against an item. The result is the same as a **negative vote,** since that item would lack a **majority.**

Two-thirds Vote—Two-thirds or more of the legal votes cast, ignoring blanks.

Unanimous Consent—(See **general consent.**)

Unfinished Business—Items not completed when the previous meeting adjourned or items postponed to this meeting from the previous one.

Viva Voce—(See **voice vote.**)

Voice Vote—Members indicate their preferences by responding with "aye" or "no." The **Chair** listens and decides which side has the **majority.** However, the **Chair** or any individual member may demand a **rising vote**, if there is any uncertainty as to the outcome.

Yeas and nays—A **roll-call vote**.

Yield—To surrender or concede to. One speaker may yield to another. A motion of lower **precedence** yields to one of higher **precedence.**

INDEX

INDEX

INDEX